by Richard C. Dewhirst, CFSP, CPC

ISBN# 978-0-9770937-1-7

Printed in Canada

"I would like to dedicate this book to the families that we care for, before, during and after they experience a loss, as well as to the memory of my grandfather, Charles F. Dewhirst Sr., without whose caring, vision, and mentoring this funeral care ministry would not have been possible."

Table of Contents

Acknowledgments

This book began nearly 20 years during a discussion with a fellow Rotarian, Claire McCarthy. About once every five years, I'd float the idea again. She'd say, "Whenever you're ready." In late fall of 2008, I was ready. I engaged her as my editor. The working process was a true collaboration. Claire and I met weekly to talk out my concepts, keeping the audience in mind. She helped me put into words what I knew intuitively. She took my original modest concept for the book and encouraged me to expand my vision to reach a greater audience. I value her professional skills as a writer and editor and appreciate our long friendship. That combination made this an enjoyable process.

Being so close to the material for so many months, it was hard to determine the answers to the most basic questions: Is it interesting and valuable? And, will people want to read it? We asked Robin Ellington, Chris Young, Clare Higgins and Ellen Higgins to review the manuscript for typos and to make general comments. Each went well beyond our expectations. They line edited and proofed copy. Their commentary was invaluable. The contributions of these pros have ensured that my message is clear and concise. Their acknowledgements validated that my advice is indeed something that is needed.

I'd also like to thank the members of the Dewhirst Family Funeral Care team. Albert Abdallah and I have worked together for the past 35 years. We grew up together and had many of the same teachers and experiences. At a time when most of those role models are now gone, Al is someone who has been there from the beginning and helps to ground and center my thinking. Sarah Stopyra, although not as "seasoned" as Al, helps me to see funeral service in new and exciting ways that I may miss or dismiss after so many years in the trenches. For her energy and enthusiasm, I am truly grateful. Sue Hill and Geri Ouellette have anchored my offices for several years. The attention to detail and the compassion with which they approach each and every family continues to impress me. They were also invaluable as proofreaders, editors and preliminary critics of the manuscript. My thanks for all they continue to add to our care team.

Finally, I'd like to thank my family. Even though they are no longer with me in physical form, my grandfather and my father still remain a constant presence in my daily life. The lessons they imparted and the power of their example drive my thoughts, feelings, and attitudes even to this day. If it were not for them this book would not have been written. I would like to acknowledge my wife Lynn, my daughter Laura and my son Rob. The life of a funeral director calls for a willingness to be there for a family in crisis whenever and wherever the need arises. Many times I was called away at times when my family may have wanted or needed me just as much as if not more than the folks on the other end of the line. The understanding and support of my immediate family throughout my career has always meant the world to me.

Preface

Why did I write this book? And why should you read it?

Death is a tough subject. I've been involved in death care services for most of my adult life, some 35 years. I've dealt with the deaths of numerous family members and countless client families. It never was an easy calling and it hasn't become easier as I've matured in the process. Along the way, I have gained quite a bit of beneficial insight and developed successful techniques and processes, which I would like to pass on to you.

Death is a mystery. I am demystifying some of the processes surrounding death. Folks have many questions, but are generally unable or unwilling to ask them. Heck, most of the time they don't even know they're entitled to ask questions of their service providers, or even what questions to pose. I am here today to tell you that yes, you can and should ask questions. Lots of them, often, and from several different sources. The great mystery to me is wondering why people don't seek out this information long before it is needed. My goals are to answer prevailing questions and to empower you to pose your own to your funeral advisor.

Not all processes are created equal, nor are funeral advisors. One advisor, for example, may have a very different way of looking at things than another. Know who and what are your options, long before a need arises.

Death is multifaceted and sometimes complicated. For all deaths there is a before, during and after. I speak to how this three-prong dynamic works and how we can get a better handle on things. One key is to be proactive and forward thinking versus the traditional reactive mode that has become the typical American mode of operation.

Even the funeral director doesn't get it right all the time. Finally, by telling some personal stories concerning the deaths of my loved ones – how things went well, how they didn't, and what I learned from the experiences – I hope to have you better understand your challenges beforehand, so you are prepared to face the inevitable.

The Circle of Life

I was born to be a funeral director. Or at least that was what everyone said to me. I was born into a funeral home family. My grandfather and my father were both funeral directors and it was assumed from the earliest age I can remember that I would carry the torch. As I was growing up it never occurred to me that there were other options. I simply fell into line and did what I was expected to do.

This is not to say that I didn't want to be a funeral director. I never knew any other way of life. Besides, I really enjoyed helping people, being in the community and continuing the long legacy of service for which my family was known. I took this responsibility quite seriously and worked very hard to become proficient in all areas of funeral service. When many of my colleagues had finished their funeral service education and got their licenses, I continued taking courses, working towards more professional certifications and trying to expand my knowledge of all facets of funeral service and affiliated professions we worked with. I wanted to know all I could, not only about my own profession but the professions of those who assisted families before, during and after the funeral process.

When I first began my career, I was primarily involved in the technical aspects of funeral service: the transfer of the deceased from the place of death, as well as the care and embalming of the body. I was a licensed funeral director in my home state of Massachusetts when, in 1982, I began a position as an apprentice in New Hampshire. This two-year process away from my family's business would allow me to obtain a New Hampshire funeral director's license in addition to my Massachusetts license. This was a rarity at the time, but my time away allowed me greater insights into funeral service than I could get by working solely with my family.

As I was now an employee, I experienced a wholly different viewpoint from working within my family. I was not the "boss's kid," now I had to pull my own weight just like anyone else. Not that I took advantage of the fact that my family owned its own business when I was back home. Just the opposite, I felt that I had to work even harder at home to "prove" that things weren't just being handed to me. My grandfather and father also never let me get away with anything just because I was family.

While working in New Hampshire, I was also just "one of the guys." Having seen funeral life from both sides of the equation gave me a greater appreciation for what support staff brings to the funeral process. I always wanted to give as much as possible to the families being served even when I was working for another funeral home. This was due to my own professional pride and I wanted each family to have the best experience possible, from the funeral home owner all the way down to the person who cleans the bathrooms. Everyone had an important role in serving that family and everyone had to be as committed as the next to make sure the whole experience was beneficial. I soon found out just how important the "hired help" could be. Often times, I would be working with a family when the boss was not around. It became my responsibility to help that family as the owner would. If I failed at my level, then it didn't matter how good a job the boss would do. The system would fail and the family would be shortchanged. This is a lesson that I try to keep foremost on my mind as well as the minds of Dewhirst Family Funeral Care team members.

Spending my early years working on both sides of the fence prepared me for my next breakthrough. I was now versed in all aspects of the interior workings of the funeral process from the funeral home status. It was now time to expand my knowledge outward to the processes of those professionals with whom we worked. These folks, for example, include the church and clergy, cemetery and crematory employees, hospital and health care personnel and state and local health agents. I wanted to know as much as I could about the people and professions who aided the funeral director when a family had a funeral care need.

As I was building up this bank of knowledge and experience, I was still missing several important components. When I first began my journey in death and funeral care, it was all about the "business" of funeral service. I was very good at business and being able to "process" families and their specific needs. I honestly thought that this was what I was supposed to do, and I was good at it. I could talk about all aspects of funeral service with anyone, at any time, in any venue necessary.

I didn't know it then but I still hadn't "experienced" funeral service.

When I speak of "experiencing" funeral service, I mean that I had not been through the process of a death myself personally. This all changed when my grandmother died in 1980 and my grandfather in 1981. Now I was on the other side of the desk. Now I was beginning to get a glimpse of what it was like for the families I was serving. I started to gain a new insight and appreciation for my client families' needs, once I walked in their shoes.

Fast forward to 1997. In the space of two years, I lost my mother-in-law, grandfather-in-law, sister-in-law and father. Now I was smack dab in the middle of what happens when we lose someone. Not only was I in the middle, I was losing family members in all generations, old, young, sick, healthy, and so on. The emotional, psychological and spiritual aspects of losing these family members had a profound effect on me as a funeral care professional.

I can say from experience, even funeral directors don't get it right. How we handled my father's illness, funeral and recovery period is a case in point.

When my dad was diagnosed with emphysema, we were all concerned with his care primarily, but not with his death. I know that human nature would have us deny the fact that we will all die one day. Under such circumstances, we should have been discussing all possible scenarios: Discussions were needed before he was diagnosed. At least if we had created a benchmark, we would have had a beginning point of reference. None having been established, we concentrated on his care and spoke nothing of the reality of his eventual death.

My dad was further diagnosed with lung cancer. His death was only a question of time. Was now the time for our family to start the planning process? Probably, but we were so involved with his immediate care that we just were dealing with things as we went along, all reactive not proactive. The problem was that as we went along, things got worse and we got increasingly emotionally and psychologically weakened by the situation.

The final blow came about when he slipped into a coma and was on life support for the last six weeks of his life.

During that time, a number of advisors were trying to get our family to make decisions about issues that could or should have been addressed in advance. At this stage of the game, we were all too drained to deal with any rational or reasonable request. His passing was a blessing. It ended suffering for him as well as for my mom and the entire family.

The funeral was a blur. Here we were, a funeral-directing family, and all we wanted to do was get through this and try to move on. I won't say that my dad's funeral was bad, but a reactive mode took over. It would have been so much better for all if we had taken the time to do a small amount of planning.

I began to examine my role as funeral director over the next few months and to process the dynamics surrounding my dad's final days. In doing so it became clear to me that I needed to look at how I help folks in a much larger context, to take on a greater mission if you will. I'm passionate about this mission for many reasons. First, I don't want what happened to my family to happen to yours.

When I first became involved in funeral service, my role was well defined and limited to taking care of dead bodies and somewhat comforting the family members left behind. My grandfather started practicing funeral service in the 1920s, my dad continued it and I followed suit. I must say we were pretty good in our specific role as immediate care provider, but we honestly didn't have a clue about what it meant to prepare in advance for a death.

Not only were we not good at preparing for death, we really were not prepared for all the fallout that happens after a death occurs. It was hard enough back when society was a lot less complicated and a lot more connected, but the need for a continuum of care in today's world is critical. We were all pretty good at funeral directing but our family was just as sorely lacking in the basic preparation and coping skills as most of the families we were serving.

Our story is not very different than those of most of the families dealing with death. The big difference is that we were supposed to be the experts! We're supposed to have this whole thing figured out and, if the funeral director is having trouble with this, what hope do average citizens have of getting things right?

The most eye-opening part of the whole experience was the period after the funeral. I had assumed that once we funeral directors efficiently took care of things, people went on their merry way and things went back to normal. Boy, was I ever mistaken.

It was bad enough to now live with the fact that my father had died and was no longer with us. Soon a whole variety of emotional and administrative issues arose. The emotional issues were greater than I had anticipated. It took me several months to work through my own grief, but longer still for several family members. I was partially prepared for this part of the post-service process. But the administrative work that had to be done – insurances, car titles, stocks, subscriptions, you name it – every time I turned around was daunting. These used to be my father's or someone else's responsibilities. No one had warned me of the minefield ahead.

Probably the most poignant part of this process, though, happened about six months after the funeral. I was having a routine conversation with my mother when all of a sudden in an exasperated voice she announced to me, "I've had it!" She then related the frustration she was feeling having to deal with a relatively minor item of my dad's estate. She then proceeded to voice frustration at the whole "mess" that she was working through and that she was having a terrible time. Sadly, several of the items were such that I could have taken care of them for her with relative ease, so I then asked her why she hadn't asked me to help her out with them. She said, "I know that you're really busy and besides, I didn't think you knew anything about this stuff." If my own mother didn't know that we help families with these issues on a regular basis, how then would anyone else know?

My father's case is the classic example of how most folks approach the whole funeral process. I didn't know what I didn't know and neither did most of the family members and friends involved in the process. It would eventually be from this and many other examples that my desire to develop and share my three-step approach to funeral care would evolve.

I began to see how my role could expand from funeral director to "funeral advisor" – someone who would be there to help families before a death occurred, would help them through the actual event, and who would be there after everyone else left to help during the recovery period that follows.

Ch.2

Start With Life

As I began to transition from funeral director to advisor, a strange thing happened. I was beginning to listen and teach more and "process" less. I started to care not so much for the goods we were providing as for the service we were rendering to those who had a need. I was expanding my work with client families to actively include advance directive planning education in the form of wills, powers of attorney and funeral wishes, and more especially, to commit to working with them long after the funeral ceremonies had concluded. Increasingly, I was becoming a resource for my families for all things funeral.

This dynamic had a profound effect on me personally. I was beginning to place a higher premium on living life to the fullest, not just on a material plane but on relationship and spiritual planes as well. Quite a bit of the work I was doing was helping families either solve problems before a death or resolve problems after a death. I began to want to do this in my own life as well. I saw how the folks that had the easiest times in transition and recovery were the ones who worked at minimizing the "stuff" that would need to be done before and after a loss. These people did as much planning as possible, knew what they wanted when the time came to deal with a death, and had good solid relationships with the family and friends around them.

Conversely, I also found that those who had the most difficult times were the ones who didn't plan, didn't know what they wanted and had less than satisfactory personal relationships.

It now became my responsibility to advise my client families about all aspects of their needs. It was also my responsibility to do as much of this for myself as possible. You see, I don't know when I'm going to die, nor do I know when those in my life will die either!

Since I came to this realization, several wonderful blessings have come into my life. My great aunt died in 2005 at age 96. She was the last of her generation. It was important for me to experience as much of her knowledge of that generation as I could before she left us. I was able over a two-year period to visit her often and soak in the stories of my grandparents' and my father's lives – stories that I would have never heard and that would have been lost to the ages had I not taken the time. I am collecting these stories of my family and my heritage and writing them down to pass along so they don't get lost after I am gone. I have become more aware of my children and I try to be as much a part of their lives as I can without becoming a pain in the neck. I'm trying to balance my life a lot more than I did when it was about work and getting ahead.

I now try to live each day as if it may be my last or the last day for someone I love. I try not to wait until it's too late to make that call, mend that fence or have that experience that I've always wanted to have. My writing, speaking and counseling have also taken on this tenor. Now when I address a group or gathering, I always start with life instead of death.

When I counsel folks on any number of funeral and death-related topics, I always ask them to consider more spiritual and deeper reasons for beginning a journey of preparation before the actual event occurs. I would ask that you also keep this in your mind as you go through the chapters to follow.

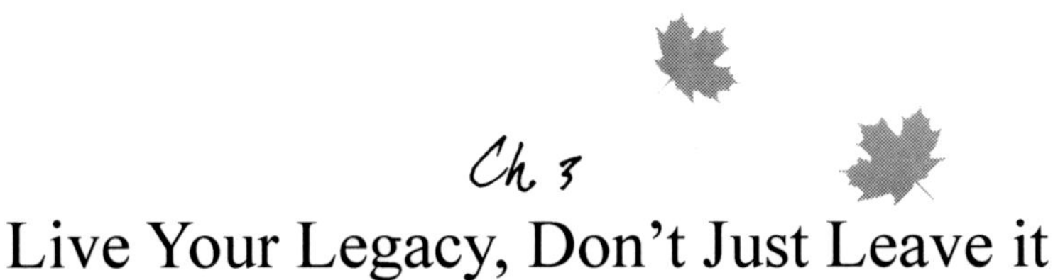

Live Your Legacy, Don't Just Leave it

I really enjoy speaking to community groups and civic and social organizations to observe the reactions they have about death and the funeral process. Quite often, if the group promotes my talk, some members are mysteriously absent because they are uncomfortable with the topic. People have flat out told me that they didn't want to hear from "the undertaker" until they needed to. The ones who do show up often do so out of morbid curiosity or out of some form of obligation to the group or organization. I will tell you, though, many folks do show up specifically because they want to know more about a topic that they view as scary and foreign – without having to visit some scary old funeral home.

People know deep down that they will die one day. They just don't want to get down and dirty with death. When I first address a group on the subject, I get a wide range of reactions. Usually the first reaction is one of humor and good-natured joking. "Oh, here's Rick Dewhirst the funeral director, you know, the last one to let you down." Or, "Look alive, here comes the undertaker."

Once I let them get all the old jokes out of their systems, I start in on breaking down the wall of denial by addressing the practical. I usually ask, "How many of you have done funeral planning before?" Typically I only get a few hands to start.

I counter with, "I bet that if we really looked at it, most everyone in the room has done some form of funeral planning and they don't even know it!" This usually gets me quite a few blank stares and questioning glances.

I then ask folks, "How many of you have wills? How many have powers of attorney, health care proxies, living wills?" Now I'm getting a lot more hands as I'm explaining to them that these are all forms of funeral planning.

I usually get the rest of the audience when I further ask, "How many of you out there have a life insurance policy? Why do we buy life insurance policies if we aren't planning on dying? You see folks, you've been thinking about your own mortality all along and you've never even realized you were doing it!" This is where I finally make the initial breakthrough needed to gain a foothold to going deeper into the subject without scaring the (pardon my wording) death out of someone.

Still, getting physically healthy people to talk about and see the value of this type of discussion is difficult at best. As easy as it is to get folks to agree that advance planning makes all the sense in the world, the only people I get anywhere with are people staring a life crisis square in the eye, people who are dealing with terminal illness, hospice situations or life-threatening surgeries.

Working with these folks has given me two major insights:
One, people who were dealing with life-ending or life-threatening situations were incredibly determined and proactive in their advance directive and funeral planning. They wanted as much information as they could get. They wanted to know as much as they could for their own benefit as well as the benefit of the family they would soon leave behind. Moreover, they wanted assurance that family members would be taken care of.

Two, people wanted the opportunity to live the rest of their lives to the fullest. This is probably the greatest gift to come out of adversity for these families. These folks knew all too well that the end time was drawing near. I personally watched as broken relationships were mended. Families that had been divided for years were coming together for support and guidance. People were taking those long put-off trips, making those neglected calls, making amends with those they hurt or, more importantly, forgiving those who had hurt them over the years. They were actually living the lives they always wanted for themselves and for those around them.

I often wondered what a blessing to have this urgency to live life to the fullest, but what a curse to have found the passion when the end was so near. How could I harness this power in my own life and then share it with as many people as possible? It helped to recall an early life lesson.

When I was 22, my grandmother died suddenly of a heart attack while walking her dog. While I was saddened by her death, my relationship with her was relatively solid and loving. I had few regrets at her passing. My grandfather, her husband, was profoundly affected by her loss and became increasingly ill. This bothered me, as he was one of my mentors. I spent a lot of time with him over the 13 months before he joined her in death. I look back now on that time as a blessing. We all knew he was failing and that time was short. Because I knew that, I made it a point to sit with him and question him on everything that came to mind – family history, funeral service, and most especially, his philosophies and feelings about life and service. At the age of 23, I didn't realize at the time that I was collecting information that I would use later in life to carry on his legacy of caring, compassion and service. I truly feel blessed for having been given that opportunity with someone so close to me.

I hear similar sentiments from many families whom I counsel. Somehow, when we know that we only have a small amount of time with someone, we tend to make the most of it. I began to think, why do we do this only when we know that someone is preparing to leave us? Why aren't we doing this on a much more regular and more concentrated basis?

Our relationships can be improved if only we stop to consider what would happen if we lost these people tomorrow. What could we do today that would make it easier on us or better for all if that person were to pass tomorrow?

Take my relationship with my dad, for example: It was often strained for a variety of reasons. I did realize that I would like things to be better before he died and I did do some work before he eventually passed.

Could I have done more? Maybe. Not now, however.

From his death, I learned that if I did have lingering issues with those still living, which could be addressed beforehand, I had a choice. I could either begin to deal with them now or wait until something happened and attempt to deal with them afterwards. Folks who lose someone before any underlying issues are resolved generally will face a nightmare. It truly is heartbreaking to see a family already in crisis during the funeral process to also have to deal with the challenge of unresolved past issues. Additionally, I have seen folks go for years – now on their own – trying to resolve issues born of denial, inability to communicate or reluctance to deal with issues that needed to be addressed while the other person was alive.

What I'm saying is, if you can begin to open those lines of communication today, it will make for an easier transition down the road after the person dies. However, that's not the only objective: The true goal is mending relationships now so that it positively affects the quality of your life from this day forward.

I have been involved in this process of observing and aiding others as well as working to improve my own relationships for years now. Moreover, it has given me a unique insight into how I look at each day.

- I have learned to take advantage of the day we are given.
- I try not to look past the present to dream about the future.
- I try not to think of today as mundane and tomorrow as all glorious and special.
- I have learned in my own life that all I really have is today. I try not to lose sight of that fact.
- Just because I have someone special in my life today doesn't guarantee that I will have him or her there tomorrow.

Based on what I have learned, I am personally determined to try to live my own life cherishing the amount of time I have left. As hard as it is, I create my own "bucket list" and work on it. This resolve has freed me up to live each day as if it may be my last. I try not to put things off: I reach out to that person I've been meaning to call and I start that exercise program I've been talking about.

However, I did not want this to be about me only or how much I could pile into life before the opportunity was gone to experience all I wanted to do before I died. I wanted it to be about how I could make it the best I could for all the people in my life whom I love and care for and who love and care for me.

Basically, I have been getting on with the business of living the life I want to live and not just settling for dreaming of the future. This attitude has allowed me to strengthen personal relationships and do things with my life that I have always wanted to do. Coming to terms with my own mortality and the mortality of those I love and care for focuses me on the fact that one day I will have the loss, but I don't have to have the regrets.

It's all about progress and not perfection. I'll never get it all right and neither will you. I don't work on it every day, but I am aware of certain dynamics in my life that if I don't get to them today, I may not get the chance to get to them tomorrow. I regularly try to work on living my legacy rather than just leaving a legacy. How about you?

EXERCISE #1
Soul-searching to examine quality of relationships and build a personal legacy:

> *"What relationships are in good shape?"*
> *"Which relationships are neglected?"*
> *"Which relationships are in need of repair?"*
> *"What could you do?"*
> *"What will you do to repair them? By when?"*
> *"Do you have a "someday" life? A wish for the future? Describe it."*
> *"What can you do today to start manifesting some of those wishes?"*
> *"What specific goals will you set?"*

Write a line for your stone or urn that sums you up:

To Do and Die or Not To Do and Die

We are a society that plans for everything. We plan weddings, birthday parties, anniversaries and special social events. We buy insurance on our cars in case an accident occurs. We purchase other types of insurance as a plan to protect us from all manner of possible problems. We plan our days, weeks, months and years. We set goals, plan vacations, have retirement plans and look to minimize risk and adversity whenever and wherever possible. All this planning helps relieve people of their fears, anxieties and feelings of helplessness.

Wouldn't it stand to reason then that we might try to plan as best we could for our death or the death of someone we love and care for? Planning for these events makes complete and perfect sense, yet people either minimize its impact or fail to plan altogether. Why do people generally avoid this at all costs? I'll share with you some of the more common reasons people give to avoid the subject. I'll also try to counter those reasons with what might happen given that particular situation. Do you see yourself in any of these five scenarios?

When I first ask why people avoid the discussion of funeral planning, some simply respond, "It's scary!" I've been working with families for 34 years and I have yet to speak with someone who was enthusiastically looking forward to the prospect of his or her own death. I'm not saying that people won't talk about it. Usually when some family member or close friend dies or gets sick, folks may begin to think about their own funeral ceremonies. At that time, they will surely be looking for someone to speak to with whom they feel comfortable and whom they hope will help them understand and address their anxiety and concern. That doesn't mean that it doesn't scare them "to death."

But what happens is that we put off a rational and open discussion on death, hoping the thought will pass and we can go back to living. Nevertheless, until one comes to grips with this issue of having to face reality, nothing gets resolved. When I work with this type of family and try to get them over the initial fear of the process, I generally ask them to consider two points:

1. I understand that talking about death may intimidate you. We'll acknowledge the fear.
2. I think it would be more helpful if we did our planning in a conceptual rather than a specific way. We don't get to specific right off the bat.

Regarding feelings, I might ask. "Do you remember how it felt the last time a death happened and no preparations at all were made? The lack of control, feelings of helplessness?" In regard to conceptualizing versus getting too specific, I ask people if having even the most basic ideas in place beforehand will soften the effect of their death or the death of someone close to them. I get folks to talk in generalities at first. I approach and discuss a wide range of topics, not necessarily hard specifics, to put people a lot more at ease. For example, rather than having a family sit right down and have me shove a casket catalogue under their nose, I simply like to put the pen down and start a simple discussion. "Could you tell me a little something about what a funeral ceremony looks like to you?" "Are we thinking about a burial service or a cremation service"? "Are we involving a church or religious community in the planning"? When we discuss concepts first, rather than specifics, we open up a more creative and unique process rather than addressing fear and avoidance.

The second reason, after "It's scary," is, "It would upset my family to know that I was even thinking about my dying." I hear this one when speaking to people about the benefits of advance directive and funeral planning. People generally think this type of planning is a good idea. Occasionally the sticking point turns out to be how the rest of the family would feel if they knew that we were actually talking about someone dying. Parents are known to remark, "My children would be too upset if they knew we were talking about my funeral." Children, on the other hand, generally want direction as to what their Mom or Dad would want for funeral services, but they don't want to upset Mom or Dad by asking them to be involved in the process. It's a standoff. Neither side realizes it and nothing gets resolved. Nobody wins.

To those folks I would say, "I'm going to assume that we agree that this would be to everyone's benefit. It would make you feel better knowing that you would be giving your family essential direction and guidance. You would also be getting the exact services that are most meaningful to you and getting them as requested, but you're telling me that it would upset your family?" I'm pretty sure that not doing some form of planning beforehand will upset them even more, especially if they get thrown into the funeral planning process at the time of death without the slightest clue as to what would be appropriate, expected or assumed!

Planning done before a death occurs is generally a smoother way to go. It's safe to say that discussion beforehand, while it at first may seem upsetting, will actually be of tremendous benefit in the long run. Moreover, as upsetting as the prospect of this talk may be, there are ways of softening the initial discussion – if the family is on the same page.

It is vitally important that everyone in a family be on the same page when it comes to advance funeral planning. The family needs to be involved in the process for it to work and to make it easier for those left behind. A family can't assume that their plans are helping someone if they don't ask their loved ones first how they need to be helped. If it is assumed that a closed casket with no viewing would make it easier for them to deal with the death only to find out that they really wanted to have an open casket and viewing, the planning is now causing more harm than good. Sometimes the best way around this is simply to leave "suggestions" or "recommendations" about wishes rather than hard and fast directives. Leaving some degree of flexibility in the planning will help when the actual funeral arrangements need to be finalized. Hopefully, as the process evolves and the rest of the family becomes more comfortable with the process, they will in turn become less fearful and more involved.

Here is a case of advance planning causing more harm than good. I was advising a woman who was planning a minimal funeral service in the hopes that it would be easier on her children. She thought that it would be easier for them to not view her body and that a funeral would not only be unnecessary but too difficult for them to go through. She simply put down her wishes without consulting with her children and announced, "Everything is taken care of, just call the funeral home when I die!" The children never really thought much about it, never got involved in the planning and never bothered to find out beforehand what Mom had planned. When Mom did die and the children gathered at the funeral home to arrange her services, they were shocked. Mom thought she was doing them a favor only to find out that the children needed and wanted more than Mom had planned. They were now feeling guilty about whether or not to honor Mom's wishes or to plan a funeral ceremony that would be helpful for them, but very different than what Mom had envisioned. The very reason that Mom did any planning at all was to help the children get over the death. By not involving them in the process, Mom actually caused more upheaval than if no planning had been done at all.

Conversely, children want to do what parents would want them to do and look for guidance in getting it right. If parents are reluctant, children are lost and frustrated. To work around these obstacles, I attempt to get proactive and begin discussions on a conceptual basis. I generally meet with the planners and give them an overview of the kinds of information and services to consider, such as burial vs. cremation and viewing or no viewing. I ask them to consider what they believe to be the best possible scenario. I then encourage them to go back to the reluctant family member and to ask open-ended questions when the right opportunity presents itself. This can happen when someone known to the family dies. "I saw that Mrs. Smith was cremated after her Mass. I'm not sure I would be comfortable with that type of service. What are your thoughts?" Or, "Bob's Mom had a closed casket at her wake. I wonder why? Do you know?"

Many ways of gathering information exist, and I generally design a strategy based on each individual family's specific needs.

Excuse number three is, "This planning business is too complicated." I often lose my audience on the perception of complexity. I have to admit that if you put everything together in one pile, this whole planning thing looks awfully intimidating. I have been doing my own planning for years, and occasionally when I look over all the planning I've done, it's mind-boggling.

Taken in small doses, funeral planning can be relatively painless and easy. Most people look at the entire elephant and think they have to eat him in one sitting! Any degree of planning is infinitely better than no planning at all. If I can at least get someone to look past the idea of having to get it all done in one sitting, we can make progress. It really is like deciding to lose 25 pounds and wanting to have it completed in two weeks. It can't be done. However, if someone begins the process and slowly makes progress toward the goal, the complicated situation breaks down into a very manageable exercise.

Once again, I simply like to begin the process by talking conceptually and working in generalities to start. It is much easier for people to talk about general ideas and concepts than sit down for a full hour of in-depth specific funeral planning. Besides, most things we discuss today may not even be that relevant five or 10 years down the road and will need to be changed anyway. It's a journey they are beginning, and not necessarily a destination that needs to be reached today. This process now becomes much more manageable and a lot less intimidating.

Fourth is, "Someone else will take care of it." Boy, are we doing our family and friends a favor with this one! I was speaking with a woman recently about the importance of organizing her funeral plans, will, health care proxy and other advance directives. She admitted to me that it was a great idea, but she didn't think she really wanted to begin the process. Having known her for quite some time I chuckled and asked, "And why not?" "Well," she said, "my children will take care of me when I die." Only half-jokingly I said, "I know your kids and do you really believe that?" She told me something that epitomizes an overriding thought process in regards to funeral planning. She said, "I had to do it for my husband and my parents. It was part of my growing up, almost a rite of passage. I didn't know what to do, but I got through it – and so will they."

I had to stop right there. Too many times in my career, I have heard the same sentiment. I had to ask her, " And how did you feel about that?" She said that it was probably one of the worst experiences that she ever had to go through. Sure, she said the funeral director was caring enough and did the best he could to get them through the death and funeral, but it was awful. She recalled having to make all the hard decisions within hours of the death, having to think about obituaries and statistical information, having to locate money for expenses and, worst of all, having to pick out a casket.

"I actually had to go into a room full of boxes for the dead and pick one out! It made me ill. I was in a fog for weeks and it took me literally months to navigate myself alone through the maze of paperwork and emotions."

Now, I had her addressing how she felt having everything just dumped in her lap. Did she really need to continue this pattern and form of abuse, or would she be willing to break the cycle and start to consider new, better and different actions? Besides, I'm thinking, we can still let the kids make some of the smaller decisions, but let's at least get some of the important stuff decided on before we involve the hesitant parties.

I allowed her to get it all off her chest and then asked, "And now you want your family to feel that way as well?"

"Of course not," she replied. Then the irony of her statement hit home. "I guess you're right," she said jokingly. "Knowing my kids, I better put it together to keep them from screwing it up!"
The fifth reason is, "I don't want to think about dying and if I don't plan it, it won't happen." This one is a little scary on many

levels. This is the kind of person who generally does no planning whatsoever. Life just seems to happen to these people and, generally, they are always reacting to life rather than living their life. I have several family members just like this. They complain that I try to have too great a handle on things. Then they moan, "Everything happens to me."

This harkens somewhat back to reason one, but is different in the respect that this person isn't avoiding the facts out of fear. They avoid facts in every aspect of their daily lives. There again, these folks have families and people in their lives who care about them. I care about my own family, but try as I may, I have to accept the fact that they aren't going to do any planning, so I do some behind the scenes planning for them. We all have people in our lives whom we worry about more than they worry about themselves.

We also assume that they are not going to change, and that's OK. That being said, whenever I run into a person in denial, I recognize I can do only so much. There again, generalization and conceptualization are my weapons in these discussions. I can't get very specific with this type of family. Let's just talk in generalities until I can get them comfortable enough to take the next steps, baby steps, but steps nonetheless. I try to find the person or persons in their lives who will be most affected by the death and encourage them to see the importance of having a plan. Once I begin discussions with the principals who will be affected, a plan of action generally can be started.

So there we have it: five reasons why people do not plan.

On the other side of the coin are the folks who do. Once they get past the initial anxiety – and we all have anxiety about death – these families discover the whole process is relatively painless, educational, somewhat interesting and, in general, it brings relief because they have initiated control over a difficult subject.

Those who are driven to do funeral planning, do so for several reasons. Sometimes it is because they are being forced into action, which can manifest in many ways. Here are five reasons folks generally begin the planning process.

1. Terminal illness. Someone will be dying. They don't really want to face it, but it's staring them in the face. They reluctantly begin the process with mixed results.
2. Monetary issues. Oftentimes when someone needs long-term care, they need to spend down their assets. They can then create a separate funeral trust to pay expenses before the money runs out. This most commonly provokes folks into action.
3. Legal reasons. Family members aren't getting along and something needs to be done. With the rising of the number of blended and non-traditional family units, these types of situations are becoming more common.
4. Families are advised that it is a wise and prudent thing to do. This generally happens when they are working with someone like me or another advisor who would be looking at the big picture. I would definitely be recommending that they get their process started as soon as possible.
5. They have decided to take control and be proactive. I do occasionally encounter people who like to take the bull by the horns, which extends to planning their own funeral. I am finding more and more aging baby boomers falling into this category.

In conclusion, the beauty of being human is that we are unique both inside and out. We do, however, share a universal experience: We are all in the process of dying. If we can face our mortality, we gain legions of opportunities to enhance our time on this earth. So I say to procrastinators, why wait?

A New Mission

I have witnessed firsthand the power of preparation, proper execution and post-service follow-through. After my father's death, my mother struggled with minor items for several months, not knowing where help was or how to get it – even though we were a funeral family! Since that awakening, it is obvious to me that all three phases of preparation need to be incorporated: before, during and after death.

The three-step process is the paramount operating principle of Dewhirst Family Funeral Care and I hope that funeral service providers will start to view their roles as threefold as well. However, before we can institute major change, we need to see where we are and where we have come from.

Indulge me as I start with a review of the traditional "during" phase, the service.

I remember a wise old funeral director once explaining the need to work with others and the need for others to work with us. In the early years of my career simply as a funeral director, it meant having a proper working relationship with a wide variety of immediate care providers. Care providers were the ones we funeral directors brought together at the time someone died to aid in the funeral services. Funeral directors usually served as coordinators or facilitators, while the other providers played their own integral part in making the service come together as a whole. Care providers include the clergy who directed the actual funeral service. Cemetery and crematory personnel aided in the final disposition of the body. Funeral assistants helped at the wakes and funeral while administrators completed paperwork, permits and obituaries. When families in need called funeral directors, they sprang into action to coordinate all elements.

After services were completed, they went back to waiting for the phone to ring to do it all over again. Occasionally, we would be asked to provide guidance in matters affecting our client families before or after a death had happened. But this was a rarity. Several seasoned funeral directors explained to me that our only duty was to be ready to serve, but to leave the before and after to others.

Since those times my funeral director role has expanded to that of an advisor who assists during all three critical phases: the preparation, the actual death along with its service rites and the post-death recovery period. Let's look at my proposed changes.

Pre-planning assures:

1. Basic components of the funeral are what is wanted and needed, and
2. Estate plans will be effectively executed.

If a family can have one central contact assisting them from A to Z, the entire experience becomes easier and much more healing and helpful. One central point of contact before, during and after a death occurs can be a true lifeline for families. This person, whether it's the funeral advisor or another point person, will check on the family after the funeral has been completed. As I mentioned in the opening pages, this was the case with my own family; the follow-through process was nonexistent.

The service today:
Social change is overdue. Funeral service providers need to be at the forefront of creating innovative services – not reacting to requests such as "just cremate me," or worse, holding on to outdated models, such as "Mother deserves the finest casket available."

Post-service recovery:
After the funeral is over, much of the support that a family had when a death occurred fades away. Everyone came together to support the family, but then life picks up and goes on. Everyone has a busy life and it's not too long after the funeral that we're caught up with our own stuff and the family is left to fend for themselves. A central contact for the family to access can also proactively check on the

family at timed intervals, critical to making certain that the family is making progress toward a return to normalcy following the death.

You may wonder, "I thought this was going on all along. Families have always had these advisors ready to help at any time the family needed them." True, the advisors were always there to help, but there are several problems with this outdated model.

Problem One: The family didn't know what they didn't know. They didn't know what they needed to do to prepare their advance directives. Sometimes they fell into it by accident or were advised on such matters, sometimes they didn't. Sometimes one advisor got part of it right, but another part of the plan was incomplete, so the whole package was lacking. A lawyer can write a great last will and testament, but if there are no other advance legal or funeral directives, the process has not been completed.

Problem Two: The advisors didn't understand the big picture. During the three separate stages, advisors may do an admirable job in regard to their particular areas of expertise; however, they really were never brought up to speed as to how their pieces of the puzzle connected with all the other pieces to make the whole. I am on a mission to help these outstanding advisors understand how to connect with other professionals and work together to create more value and more complete plans for client families.

It's imperative that we relay the importance of

- preparing for the death before it occurs,
- considering the dynamics of the funeral process and
- understanding that post-service follow-through is just as important – if not more important – than the first two components.

Thirty-four years later, I'm still waiting to find that certain "other" who can pull the whole process together so families looking for help and information have a one-stop contact for all their death care needs. To my mind, the funeral advisor is the most likely candidate.

The Changing Role of the Funeral Service Advisor

My own journey has taught me that death is complicated. Death never comes when you expect it. There is never a “right time” for someone to die. It is never really an easy or simple process. Whether we are talking about the period before someone dies, the actual funeral ceremony itself or the adjustment and recovery period after the ceremony, challenges abound. These challenges may be physical, emotional, financial, psychological, or a combination of several of these factors. I know that I have personally experienced all of these dynamics at one time or another. I successfully have helped countless clients and families work through these conditions. I continue to build and fine-tune my process to this day.

My three-step death care process includes preparing for the loss, surviving the death, and recovering after the ceremonies have been completed.

I can’t emphasize enough the importance of recognizing the three distinct parts to the process of coping with death. I also stress that these three components are intertwined. In other words, in many ways all three parts work together. By being scrupulous in planning subsequent steps, the other areas will tend to become less complicated and will blend more effectively. If we are diligent in the planning phase, then the actual death phase will be generally more fulfilling and less traumatic. If we have done the proper amount of work on the front end, then the recovery period should be less difficult and shorter in duration. Conversely, if a family chooses not to do the work on the front end, they run the risk of adding complexity, frustration and emotional turmoil.

As a funeral advisor, I am constantly looking at the overall total picture. When I am meeting with a client family, I am not only concerned with their immediate needs, but I am identifying potential problem spots that have not yet manifested. A meeting to establish advance directives can often solve this. The family has questions, concerns and fears to be identified and dealt with, and it is my job to identify immediate concerns and identify future steps.

For example, I met with one family that wanted to do a simple funeral trust. Mom was going into a nursing home and was advised to create a funeral trust and put money aside for expenses so not to jeopardize her health care benefits. The family was not aware that we could include many budget items such as cemetery and newspapers costs as well as church and clergy expenses. If I hadn't discussed the possible expenses that needed to be included in her trust, the likelihood of the family needing to come up with additional funds at the time of death would have been an ambush. Uncovering possible future needs prevented serious financial shortfalls. This "big picture" thinking headed off potential problems the family would encounter, not only when Mom died, but also during the recovery period.

Here is another case. I was working with a young lady and her dad, doing advance planning for his funeral needs. His daughter was the primary caregiver and had taken care of Dad for several years after her Mom had died. She had a brother who was disconnected from the family. The two siblings had not spoken since their mom passed away and the rift deepened over the following years. There was plenty of resentment, feelings of abandonment and apprehension in the daughter's tone. I listened more than anything else, and allowed her to release some of the pent-up frustration and tension that she had been holding onto for quite some time. When all was said and done, I gently suggested that we might want to take a closer look at this dynamic. I acknowledged that we could let it go and deal with it when the time came, but that we may want to slowly begin to address some of the concerns before we threw the emotions and complications of the actual death into the mix. She thought it might be a good idea to try to rebuild some of the relationship before Dad died but didn't know how. I suggested that maybe we could use an intermediary, another family member both sides were comfortable with to begin discussions. We might also consider using Dad's attorney as a way to begin the process.

She elected the option with which she was most comfortable and eventually lines of communication were established so that healing of the relationship could take place. Not only was this beneficial for the two siblings, but Dad was happy that his two feuding children were at least attempting to bury the hatchet. This helped them immensely when the father did die, as well as during the recovery period after the ceremony. The situation was not fully resolved, but beginning the healing process before Dad died definitely made the funeral and recovery period a lot easier to handle.

Often families will stumble into the funeral process in a fog. They have either been in denial about an impending death or were faced with an immediate care situation out of the blue. Addressing problems during the actual funeral process sooner rather than later can aid in either the recovery or advance planning stages of the process. Certainly if a family had not done any or only minimal advance planning, the possibility of helping that family with the planning component in the future now becomes likely. Identifying family dynamics and grief issues early on also helps in recovery and advance directive planning.

I am in regular contact with my client families for up to a year or more after the death has occurred just to make sure people are OK and getting the help that they need. I can't begin to tell you how many families are either paralyzed after a death or just don't know which way to turn. The phone feels like it weighs 500 pounds and they just don't ask for help. If I am in regular contact, however, I can usually determine if people are on the right road to recovery or not. As I help folks navigate through the recovery period oftentimes we begin again the discussion of being prepared for future funerals.

The recovery process also affords us opportunities at proactive problem solving. As I have mentioned earlier, no matter where we are in the process, there are always opportunities for continued improvement. Often the period of recovery for a family is not only one of healing but one in which they are acutely aware of the need to plan more effectively in the future. I am constantly on the lookout during this time to help a family identify needs and make necessary corrections and improvements. I have often found that working with families at this time is the most rewarding and most satisfying. To be able not only to help a family in crisis navigate safely through this time, but also to help them achieve a higher sense of confidence and security has always been of primary importance to me.

Once again, it's important to remember that this is a living process. We are either conscientiously or unconscientiously working on these very issues on a regular basis whether we realize it or not. It has become my passion and mission to help clients to understand this dynamic and, with my assistance, to continue to make progress in what is arguably the most difficult process that any of us will ever have to face.

Selecting the Right Funeral Advisor

Often, when I first meet folks and they ask what I do for a living, they are taken aback when I say I am a funeral care advisor. "You mean an undertaker?" they ask. I say, "So to speak." The rest of the conversation typically goes like this:
"Gee, you don't look like an undertaker."
"Oh, what's an undertaker supposed to look like?"
"Well you know, kind of gaunt and morbid, dressed in black, you know."

I guess most people who don't know someone in the funeral profession might have this stereotype somewhere in their head, thanks to cartoons and movies.

The reality is that if you don't personally know who will be helping you when you need funeral care guidance, you may end up with someone who, although he or she may be licensed to provide services, may not be the person you will be most comfortable with. This is why it is critically important that you establish some sort of relationship with a funeral care professional before you are thrown into a situation that can be made so much worse if you're working with someone you're not happy with, or not completely able to trust or have confidence in.

As I have stated repeatedly, advance planning is so critical in making these difficult times and decisions easier. Part of this planning exercise is to find, in advance, someone trustworthy, who makes you feel comfortable. The person you eventually end up working with will be helping you at an extremely difficult time. You will probably want someone who is knowledgeable in all aspects of funeral care planning before the death happens. You will want someone who can manage the actual funeral ceremony and cares on a very human level

– first – about you and your family. In addition, you want someone who will be with you after the ceremony concludes to help guide and walk with you as you work to pick up the pieces after everyone else has returned to their own lives. Some funeral care advisors can overlook these serious and sincere considerations.

Consider several attributes in your selection of a funeral care advisor. Does your funeral director:

> *"Have a deep history in the community?"*
> *"Give back to the community in terms of volunteer and betterment efforts?"*
> *"Have professional certifications including certified funeral service practitioner (CFSP) or certified preplanning consultant (CPC)?"*
> *"Continue to learn through industry courses and conferences and has assumed any leadership roles in the profession?*
> *"Demonstrate interest and knowledge in other areas associated with funeral care?"*
> *"Advise you on the aspects of preplanning as discussed in prior chapters, with not only their charges in mind but also the additional services that may be required?"*
> *"Walk with you after everything is said and done?"*
> *"Have knowledge in post-service follow-through?"*
> *"Encouraged you to be proactive in your advance directive planning, and are they confident enough to suggest and help you do more research if needed with other funeral providers?"*
> *"Exhibit creativity and provide alternatives you may need?*
> *"Get you the services you request rather than tell you what you can't have or shouldn't do?"*
> *"Encourage you to share your thoughts and plans with your family, and are they willing to assist you in this exercise?"*
> *"Make house calls and make you as comfortable as possible in all areas of service?"*

Another area that you may choose to explore is that of secondary expertise. Does your funeral advisor have knowledge in other areas such as legal, spiritual, estate planning, financial, grief counseling? Even though your advisor may not be an attorney, grief counselor, estate planner or CPA, he or she may have enough basic knowledge to save you several hundreds of dollars in professional fees.

I'm not suggesting your funeral advisor give professional advice when it is clear that a proper professional should be consulted; however, there may be times when an enlightened funeral advisor may be able to advise you in several ways other than direct funeral knowledge. Just another area you may want to check into!

Truthfully, when everything is said and done, the one thing you need to ask yourself is, "Do I feel comfortable with this person and do I trust them to get me through this difficult time?"

Ch. 8

Drafting the Complete Advisor Team

Who needs to be on the team, what to look for in advisors and how to get them to work together in your best interest.

As I have mentioned in the previous chapters, there are many different components to putting proper advance planning directives in place. The way most people go about it is generally hit or miss. They go along their merry way until some life event happens either to themselves or to a family member or close friend. At that point, they either are forced into making decisions, or they think it would be a good idea to do something about their own situation based on an event that happened to someone close to them.

Reacting emotionally has its flaws.

If people take action because a decision needs to be made and made now, they generally just take the first solution handed to them without any real thought or study. This leads to many problems, including:

- not getting all the facts
- picking the wrong advisor
- paying too much and
- not completely fixing the problem, thereby increasing the chance it will arise once again

Two, procrastination sets in. I know for me that if I am faced with having to make decisions that I know are good for me but ones that I'm not thrilled about actually making, I'll find a way to put it on the back burner until I either forget about them or they go back to being problem number one. The cycle then repeats itself until the problem or issue actually gets addressed. Over the years in my role as facilitator, I generally become for most people the "fly in the ointment." I become the person who initiates the discussion about all manner of advance directives. I then become the person who continually works with folks on getting things done, putting them in place and regularly fine tuning them until they are needed.

My role as facilitator is to create and work with the family's advisor team. It is very important that I work closely with the family to identify the proper advisors, ones they are most familiar with, and coordinate services well before their help is needed. Once we determine the needs of the family and all directives are in place, we can monitor the plan regularly and identify updates and changes. Advisors who know their jobs well can also anticipate problems. We help to prevent the procrastination factor. I came about this process rather painfully and by many years of trial and error. I hope to save my clients this problem going forward.

Who needs to be on the advisor team? As facilitator/funeral director I have worked with many advisors over the years. Every family has their own unique needs. Some families need several kinds of advisors and some need only a certain few. I work individually with each family to help them decide what advisors they need and we work together to identify the right ones for the job. I have obtained advisors for families years after the original plans were first put into place who were not needed until much later in the process.

Regardless, the plan can and should be ever evolving, and we are free to add and subtract from the team as needed. Over the years, I have found that most families need to begin with five advisors:

- facilitator/funeral director
- legal counsel
- spiritual advisor
- insurance advisor
- CPA or estate planner

I generally serve as facilitator for my client families. Any advisor can act as facilitator if he or she can manage others to work as a team. I try to not get caught up in egos. If a family prefers another advisor to be facilitator rather than me, then so be it. I am also not embarrassed to point out to that family if and when the advisor/ facilitator doesn't appear to be acting in their best interests. This happens often because most advisors are great at providing their piece of the pie but aren't set up to coordinate the whole affair. I am experienced enough to provide the funeral component but I regularly coordinate all associated needs.

Typical questions you may have include:

"What types of things do my advisors need to provide?"

The facilitator needs to be able to understand the Big Picture: What are the total needs of the client family, how can these needs be addressed and who needs to be involved? The funeral director provides the actual funeral piece and all offshoots of that particular process.

The legal advisor provides counsel on wills, powers of attorney, health care proxies, living wills, probate, etc.

The spiritual advisor addresses the spiritual emotional and psychological needs of the client family.

The insurance advisor provides insight into insurance needs – health, life and disability.

The CPA or estate planner provides answers to financial questions, taxes, liabilities and the like.

"What are some of the things that I need to look out for when choosing an advisor?"

Consider several warning signs to watch out for during an interview with an advisor. Yes, I said interview. Too often I have had families pick an advisor without really interviewing them. After working with them for a while, the relationship, for whatever reason, just doesn't seem to feel right. The client feels guilty that they are deep into the process and they don't want to hurt the advisors feelings. They feel awkward about admitting that the relationship isn't really working, but they plow ahead and try to suck it up hoping it will get better. What generally happens is that no one wins. The advisor doesn't realize the relationship is flawed and the client detaches from the process. This deprives the client of services they want and need and the whole system either stalls or fails. I have helped my client families remove themselves from these advisor relationships and identified better advisors for a more fulfilling experience. Advisor relationships are a lot like personal relationships. They do need to feel right and they can be changed if needed.

"Are there several common areas of concern to watch out for in an advisor relationship?"

"Is the advisor only interested in his or her piece of the puzzle?" This is, after all, a team effort. There are many components that make the whole. If an advisor is solely interested in their piece of the puzzle and not the others, watch out! Their lack of cooperation generally means it's all about the money and not about the client.

"Is the advisor part of a large corporate structure where you are to be simply processed according to corporate policy?"

"Is the advisor sensitive to your particular needs, and will he or she be equally as helpful whether he or she is helping you with something that will not give them a direct return?"

"Does the advisor give you and your needs the proper respect and attention?"

"Do they have enough time to really know and understand your wants and needs?"

These are all valid and legitimate questions. You want people on your team who are advocating for your interests. Advisors who will help families choose wisely and thoroughly.

I have worked with all kinds of advisors, and when you work with as many as I have, you get to know the ones who will really be there when the chips are down. One particular situation that comes to mind involved a family that I worked with some years ago. I received a call for a woman who said she had a particularly challenging situation. Her brother had been a homeless person and had been addicted to drugs and alcohol. He had died on the streets, and his body was brought to a local funeral home. She had visited the funeral home to see what could be done to provide simple services for her brother. No one had any money and the brother was totally destitute. The funeral director at the time was busy with several full-paying customers. This family was obviously an inconvenience to him and they sensed that from the very beginning. They walked out of the funeral home with little hope of a solution, unless they could come up with a substantial amount of money. They had tried to call for government assistance. They spoke to two lawyers about what could be done. Because of the circumstance, no one was really interested in helping. I invited the woman to meet with me to see what could be done. We spent two hours going over what needs there were (the brother had minor children) and what we could do to help. I was able to connect this woman with the proper government agencies that would provide relief for her immediate needs. I was also able to connect her with a sympathetic lawyer who would handle the legal issues at an affordable rate. I arranged for a spiritual advisor as well as several social services agencies to help with the emotional issues.

Within two hours, I was able to put this family back on track with all the advisors and services that they would need. This woman has since become a close friend. I helped create an advisor team for her personal needs as well as those of several of her family and friends. That team also includes the kindly lawyer and spiritual advisor. It is critical that the proper team be identified, put into place and put to work before the needs arise.

OK, So What Do We Do in Advance?

At the core, this chapter is about what to know before you go – because you want to ensure that your family is free to grieve versus conduct undone business during the days following your death. Your funeral advisor is your point person to walk you through – in advance.

When I'm out in the community I get some of my best reads as to what "death questions" people are thinking about. Usually, it is a much more relaxed setting that invites folks to gently pull me aside and begin to ask me about all sorts of things. Burial versus cremation. Open versus closed casket. Do I need to be embalmed? How much does it cost? The list is endless. People do want to know about this stuff but are still afraid to ask, or don't know how to ask. This is really a shame. I have tried over the years to break down the stigma that surrounds discussing death in a healthy proactive way. I've made a lot of progress but we still have work to do.

In this chapter, I hope to touch on the four main areas of funeral planning: organizing statistical data, planning the funeral ceremony, customization of the services and the obituary, and expenses. Some areas are treated in detail in later chapters. These areas are easy to facilitate before someone has died but can get very complicated if left until the last minute. Here we go.

AREA ONE: ORGANIZING STATISTICAL DATA

Statistical data needs to be organized primarily to complete a death certificate as well as to complete other legal paperwork such as Social Security forms, Veteran's forms and insurances. This one area is so benign that every person should have this information on file with a trusted advisor as a bare minimum. This information is so easy to assemble before something happens that it absolutely makes no sense not to have it ready to go. It would be as if someone were heading off on a trip with no passport, no directions and no confirmation numbers. You are, after all, heading off on the ultimate trip and to not have the basics in place before you depart is senseless. If someone were interested in only beginning the advance arrangement process, this is where we need to start.

Information needed – and often gathered incorrectly if left to the last minute – include date and place of birth, social security number, education, veteran's discharge papers, occupation, employment and type of work done, parents' names with mother's maiden name, and place of birth.

The biggest problem we have is that once a person is gone, and if the remaining family members did not really know where this information was kept, the chances of error grow exponentially.

And on an emotional level consider this: When a death happens it is not the time to be playing Dick Tracy! It's time to be reflecting on the loss, embracing family and celebrating the life of the person who has passed. Unfortunately, all too often, the funeral team needs to keep the initial focus on data collection. To understand the complications associated with incorrect or missing information, consider the following possible outcomes.

Maybe we aren't able to file the death certificate, so we have to postpone services or disposition until we can get everything straight. Maybe the death certificate is wrong or not completed, so we can't get certified copies, which means we can't apply for insurances or benefits and then we have no access to money. Maybe we can't file for veteran's benefits, military honors or social security benefits until we have our data in place.

I have worked with too many families who, on top of all the other stuff they need to deal with, would have been so much farther ahead of the curve if they only had this little bit of planning in place.

AREA TWO: PLANNING THE FUNERAL CEREMONY
Our next logical step is to begin discussion on the planning of the actual ceremony. This generally involves the date, time and place of the actual service but also the discussion of calling hours (a wake if you will) and type of disposition, be it burial or cremation. Here again, just a little bit of advance planning can make all the difference in the world. How easy it is beforehand to weigh out all the options regarding location of service. Begin with asking these questions:

"Do we need to involve a church community?"
"Do we need to hold services at a funeral home?"
"On the other hand, do we need to think a little creatively about an alternative site for services?"

Having this discussion beforehand can open up myriad possibilities for a meaningful and well-planned tribute. When a family is turned upside down, it is darn near impossible to try to create something of meaning and substance. You see, I've dealt with families who have and haven't planned. The families who planned had the chance to really think this out and work with me to create a very special and unique ceremony. The folks who didn't take the time to plan simply wanted me to get them through the loss as best I could. They were in no emotional or mental state to really try to focus on what choices they had or what would make sense. They simply wanted me to help them make the pain go away.

I've always tried to do the best I could but I know that we can do so much better. That is probably why I get so passionate about advanced planning. It not only helps the family, it helps me help the family. No one should be guessing at a time like this. I want to know that what I'm about to do for this family is what is really going to be helping them not only at the immediate time but also as they move forward.

In some ways the discussion on calling hours, open or closed casket, flowers or memorials and pallbearer choices, is simply easier when it is done sooner rather than later.

The most confusion surrounds the discussion of burial versus cremation. I get families all the time who wait until someone dies to try to figure out "Did Dad want to be buried or cremated?" I've seen family members literally fighting over which way to go.

Many valid reasons exist for choosing either method of final disposition, but when a family is in emotional crisis, it is not the best time to try to reason it out. These simple areas of concern as you can see are relatively easy to facilitate before hand, but can become a real bear at immediate need.

AREA THREE: CUSTOMIZING THE SERVICE AND OBITUARIES

These activities can be very healing and creative if sketched out beforehand. An obituary can be so much more than just a short, sterile biographical sketch of a person's superficial existence.

Taking the time to really think out what needs to be expressed about the life of the person – who they were, what made them tick, what were their passions – these are the nuances of powerfully written tributes.

If left until the last minute, an obituary simply notifies the community of a person's death, family members listed, and ceremonies planned. A well-thought out newspaper tribute lets the reader know who that person really was. It is the family's chance to tell the story of a person they loved and cared about. Put some loving attention and thought into it.

Planning meaningful funeral ceremonies can also be extremely powerful if done with clear thinking in place.

> *"What kind of readings do you want to include?"*
> *"What kind of music would be appropriate?"*
> *"Who needs to speak and be involved?"*
> *"Who will write and who will deliver the eulogy?"*
> *"What other special touches do you want to include to make this funeral different than all the other funerals we have attended?"*

I've seen incredible things done when a little advanced planning is put into place. We performed a service for a music lover in a world-renowned music hall. We did a celebration of life at a local restaurant with all the components of the funeral – and the after-service luncheon all at the same location. We've done some incredibly thoughtful and memorable scattering of ashes following cremation at the ocean, in parks, in the mountains, with or without a ceremony.

Over the past few years, several church communities I am involved with have recognized the increase in the selection of cremation by their member families. In many cases, these family members were long-time church members and the church was a meaningful part of their life story. As more and more folks chose cremation rather than burial, the discussion of what to do with the cremated remains increasingly became an issue. These church communities started to receive requests to scatter some or all of a person's ashes on or around the church grounds, grounds that had such significance in their lives. As these requests grew, the churches started to look into designating areas for memorial scattering gardens for use by members and friends of the church. I have assisted several churches directly in the creation of such gardens and scattering areas. Not only are these areas very attractive and peaceful, they provide a meaningful place for a family to scatter the ashes of that family member in a very appropriate setting.

AREA FOUR: EXPENSES

Here is the granddaddy of all the areas that absolutely needs to be addressed before a death actually occurs. Of all the questions I get out in the field, the majority revolves around the cost of funeral goods and services. We have three areas of concern here.

- One, if you don't know what you want then how can I tell you what it's going to cost?
- Two, we need to know all necessary components to build a true budget. And
- Three, where is the money going to come from?

So often people want to know what it's going to cost them. They don't know what they want and they aren't sure how they're going to pay for it. Lovely! I could make it easy on them and myself by just suggesting that they put away 20 grand; I'll figure it out at the time for them and give them back any money they didn't spend. A better way in my opinion would be to sit down and figure our what the person or family would like or will need when a death occurs. I can then create several scenarios with several budgets for discussion. Finally, together we can then figure out how those costs are going to be taken care of.

Everyone I have taken through this process beforehand has found it not only to be easier and more fulfilling than if they had waited until a death had happened, but they also feel more in control and much less anxious and fearful of coping when the death actually occurs.

The choice is yours: deal now from a position of pro-activity, strength and confidence or deal later from a position of fear, anxiety and vulnerability. My choice would be now and I hope yours is as well.

It's a Nightmare Without Directives

When I speak with a family about advance directives folks generally smile politely and nod, but I know that I'm going to have to do some explaining before they really understand how crucial advance directives can be.

Advance directives come in tangible forms such as last will and testament, powers of attorney, health care proxies, living wills, and death care planning. (They come in non-tangible, subtle ways as well. "Emotional directives" are discussed in the next chapter.)

Several years ago, a woman called me to make an appointment to discuss her mother's funeral arrangements. Her mom was a resident of a local nursing home. Mom had taken a turn for the worse and the folks at the nursing home had recommended that she discuss final arrangements as soon as possible. This was a positive start to advance planning but unfortunately for the family they were coming to me very late in the game.

Mom had been in the nursing home for several years, first as a private pay resident then when all her money had been spent, her expenses were covered by state and federal assistance. I sat with this woman and we discussed what would be appropriate for Mom's services when she did die. She said that she always assumed we would do the same for Mom as we had done for Dad. I said that that was a common way to approach funeral planning.

We looked back to see what services were done for her father and I set about to duplicate them at today's cost. Those same services today would be about $10,000. The woman agreed that we were in line with what she assumed, the only problem was that Mom had spent all her money at the nursing home and now only had $2,000 to her name. She said she would need to go to her two brothers and her sister to see how they wanted to handle the expenses. We arranged to meet in a week and discuss the matter further.

A week later, we met again, but this time the woman was extremely distraught. In speaking with her siblings, she found no consensus. One brother who was estranged from the family didn't care what they did and wasn't going to be involved. Her sister was very supportive and sympathetic to the situation but was going through a divorce and was not able to help financially. Her other brother could help only a little and questioned the need for such an elaborate service. He also felt that as the oldest child, he should have the final say in the matter.

You see, no funds were put aside for final expenses and no will drawn naming the administrator of Mom's estate when she died. There were some papers established years earlier, but they had all named Dad as the ultimate decision maker. Dad had been gone for years and his name had never been taken off any of the documents! Thus began a nasty battle over money, control, and decisions. That alone was bad enough, but the intangible or subtle directives became even worse.

Mom had slipped badly and was in no way capable of giving direction or insight into how she would like things to be handled. Arguments ensued over everything from routine expenses, to who would get Mom's Hummel collection, to what music would be played at the memorial service. By the time everything was said and done, no one was speaking and the family dynamics would be damaged for months if not years to come.

Had this family known that they could have done most of this planning earlier and at a time when Mom could be involved in the process directly, the outcome would have been very different. In a case like this, I can suggest several areas where we could have improved the process.

When Dad died was the perfect time to start addressing Mom's situation. Not necessarily right after the funeral, but at the time when the family is doing all the post -funeral paperwork. At this time, I like to get the paperwork filed; and assist the family as they return to a sense of normalcy.

- We could have spoken about the need to review all documents to make sure that Dad's name was removed and that the appropriate child's or children's names be put in place.
- We could have established new documents to list who should be involved in health care decisions, financial decisions, etc.
- We could have started a discussion of Mom's funeral plans as well with just a simple folder to start.
- We could have prepared for the time when Mom would go into a nursing home, and during the spend-down period we could have protected the money the family would need to pay all funeral expenses.
- We would have been able to put aside money in a qualified funeral trust to pay all expenses, rather than wait until it was all gone to try to figure out how we would pay the bills.

Communication is key in making sure folks get through this process in the best possible way. Leaving things to chance is never the right way to go.

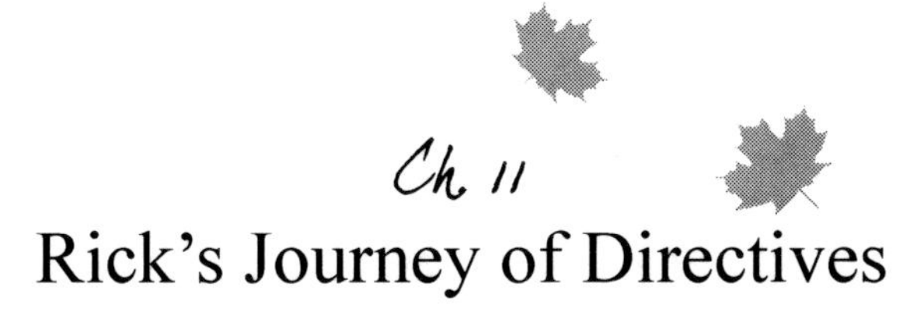

Rick's Journey of Directives

Advance directive planning, my friends, is a journey. Most folks I speak with initially think that once they do advance planning, it's done for good. That could not be further from the truth.

When I first got married and had children, I personally started my own advance directive journey. My wife and I first met with an attorney more than 20 years ago when our first child was born. At that time we needed wills, powers of attorney, health care proxies and living wills. We wanted to know that in the event of a tragedy when our children were too young to take care of themselves, our wishes would be met. We made the appropriate decisions and named the appropriate people to handle our affairs in the event one or both of us would die prematurely. As intimidating as it was for both of us to face these decisions, it was a tremendous weight off our shoulders.

Once we had those directives in place, we also sat down together and discussed how our funerals would be handled. As morbid as it may seem, we actually had fun with some of the crazy things we envisioned for our services. We filed everything away and went on with the business of living.

I didn't really give it all that much thought until about five years later. I received a call from my attorney asking to arrange a meeting to review the documents from five years earlier. I looked over the documents and noticed a few minor changes that needed to be made and let him know. Nothing major, but not a bad idea to just dust off the old documents and bring them up to date.

We also did the same for our funeral plans. They also were still pretty much relevant and needed little review. The real eye-opener came at the 10-year mark. Once again I was busy with the business of living when I got the reminder call from my attorney about a review. This time though, much more had changed. Two people that were mentioned in my directives had died since the last review. We now needed to remove them from the documents and put new ones in place. Not only that, but one family member had become unreliable due to health matters, and that needed to be changed as well. If something had happened and these changes had not been made, even though we had the proper documents in place, those outdated documents actually would have caused more harm than good.

We also needed to review our funeral plans for ceremony and disposition. Once again our eyes were opened. I had originally planned on being buried in a family lot. My thinking had changed since the initial plan and I now wanted to be cremated. My wife remarked that she never knew that I had changed my mind, and if I hadn't mentioned anything she would have buried me like the original plan had directed. We both got a little chuckle over that one, but both of us readily admitted that it really helped us to review this on a regular basis.

This is my particular example of the "journey" of the advance directive. We review our plans every five years. A lot has changed and evolved over the past 20 years, and we have made a conscious effort to keep up with those changes.

I know firsthand that planning isn't just a punch list. Planning isn't just something we do once and that's it. Planning is a verb, not a noun. Planning is a process, one that has a beginning and an end but one where the process is in the journey. A journey that I take myself and with my client families every step of the way.

Ch. 12

How Much Does It Cost and Who Will Pay?

I routinely am asked the question, "How much does a funeral cost?" This comes up more than any other topic – and with good reason. Funeral costs can range anywhere from several hundred to many thousands of dollars, depending on the desires and circumstances of that individual or family. It's similar to asking how much a wedding costs. How can wedding planners and vendors estimate the cost without knowing some details such as, are you eloping or are you doing the whole open bar with the one-month honeymoon? As with a wedding, the only way to prepare a true and legitimate funeral budget is by working closely with an enlightened advisor.

When it comes to budgetary issues, I define an enlightened funeral advisor as one who

- Asks you what you think you want rather than telling you what you need;
- Is savvy enough to know enough about true trusts to introduce you to the concept, but honest enough to admit he or she isn't a financial advisor (see next chapter on trusts), and
- Can patiently guide you through the myriad of changing funeral options in today's contemporary society.

Due to cultural, religious and social changes, funerals come in all shapes and sizes. Therefore, costs are dependent on the needs and wants of the individual. What one person would consider a funeral expense – say buying flowers for the service or publishing an obituary – would not be a consideration of another. Funeral expenses are more than simply a casket and services. They include a range of expenses that are unique to the ceremony that you and your family will deem appropriate at the time.

I feel it is essential that we begin exploring budget concerns by first discussing the planning process in wide generalities. I do most of the initial planning with my clients as a general discussion on what a funeral ceremony means to them.

> *"What components does it need to include?"*
> *"What services will be brought into play?"*
> *"Who or what needs to be involved?"*
> *"What does the ceremony need to look like?"*
> *"Will there be a wake/visitation?"*
> *"Will the body be present and will the casket be open for viewing?"*
> *"Will there be a funeral ceremony and will a clergy or church community be involved?"*
> *"Will we be choosing burial or cremation and, if we choose cremation, what will be the final disposition of the cremated remains?"*

Once we get a general idea of where a family appears to be headed in the process, I can begin to create scenarios and budgets that will suit their wants and needs. These plans can be very simple and only cost several hundred dollars (cremation and no service) or stretch to very elaborate celebrations that require budgets well into the thousands.

However, don't just take my word for it.

It has always amazed me that intelligent people will shop all kinds of goods and services as a matter of course. However, when it comes to funeral goods and services they just dive in headfirst and hope they don't break their necks.

In today's day and age, it's not only prudent but also advisable to shop around – not only for price, but to find the right funeral director. I repeat, funeral relationships need to work on both a fiscal and personal level. You need to feel good about what you are paying as well as the person getting your check. And this is why I devoted an entire chapter to helping you define a good working relationship with your funeral advisor.

The average family has the need to purchase funeral goods and services on average once every seven years. Every seven years! Even if you had a good experience the last time you needed to involve a funeral home, a lot can change in seven years. Maybe that kindly old gentleman who helped you last time is gone. Maybe someone with a different philosophy bought out the firm you worked with last time. Any number of scenarios could present themselves.

The one thing I always mention to families is that it's important to know what your costs are going to be before a death has occurred. There have been situations more numerous to count where a family thought they knew what the funeral was going to cost, but were in for a rude awakening. It is all too common that people don't have any clue as to the extent of necessary funeral expenses. These folks get well in over their heads and the challenge for me is to make sure that they get what they want and need without drowning in debt. I always advise people to research an estimate of costs either beforehand or at the time a death occurs.

"Get an estimate?" you say. "How can I get an estimate? I thought when a person died you just called the funeral home and it just costs what it costs. I didn't know you could get estimates or even ask questions for that matter."

It frequently happens that families didn't know that they had this option. The reality is that you can absolutely get estimates even after a person has died, and with no obligation to the funeral home providing the estimate. When a person dies, most folks aren't in the best emotional state of mind. They didn't think that they could price shop several funeral homes, nor do they really feel like doing it after someone has died. The fact remains that unless you really like your funeral director or local funeral home, it's always a sound idea to have several comparisons for like services.

If your local funeral director is hesitant to provide information it should cause a red flag to go up in your mind. Turn to the funeral director or funeral home that is most open with information and advice.

If a funeral director is only talking to you about the casket and his or her services and not looking at all the expenses in addition to the funeral home, fees, additional problems may result.

You need to be working with someone who will help you establish a budget that includes all true costs, and not just those of the funeral director. Those costs take the form of items such as cemetery, crematory, flowers, church fees, newspaper obituaries, travel expenses and caterers.

Another reason to shop around is that individual funeral providers' costs can vary significantly. One funeral home may be able to provide less expensive services because they have a lower overhead than the provider down the street. Maybe one funeral home does more business than another, and because of economies of scale, they can provide quality service at a more reasonable price. Maybe one provider has a philosophy of higher price than the guy down the street. Maybe one provider is part of a corporate network that has a higher cost basis than a local family-owned firm. Or vice versa. Services and philosophies can vary significantly and you need to be aware in order to make an informed decision.

A Tisket, A Tasket, Let's Talk About A Casket

One of the biggest expenses can be the casket. Caskets can range from only a few hundred dollars to many thousands of dollars. The wide range is due to construction considerations, including materials used (cardboard for direct cremation, to metal or wood for a more traditional service) and embellishments and customizations such as hobby plaques to original works of art. But buyers beware: Funeral directors acting as brokers have carte blanche ability to mark up wholesale prices. Bear in mind, you can shop around and compare retail prices. Although most people find it impractical, you can deal directly with a wholesaler and have the casket drop shipped to the funeral home. I bet you didn't know that you can also rent a casket for the wake if the disposition is to be cremation.

Additionally, it is crucially important to understand that most funeral service providers have access to hundreds of casket choices. You may be shown only a dozen or so in a "selection room." These may represent a range of available choices – or they may represent what the funeral provider wants you to buy. As this is a very scary process for most family decision-makers, it's important to point out that more options exist beyond those that have been presented. Ask pointed questions concerning options. This is always easier to do sooner rather than during a time of duress and loss.

Now on to how to establish budget details. When discussing funeral expenses I always encourage a family to try to write down all the costs that they feel will need to be addressed at the time the death occurs. Most often they hit the obvious ones, but miss many of the more subtle expenses such as monument engraving, church charges, musician fees and travel expenses.

I encourage you to answer this two-part question: What items are non-negotiable and, based on those items, how will you finance your arrangements? Personal savings? Survivors chip in? Life insurance policy? A funeral trust? The next chapter is devoted to educating you about the concept of funeral trusts.

Funeral Preplanning and a True Funeral Trust

First, let's clear up one huge misconception: Funeral preplanning does not equal funeral prepaying. Creating a funeral trust is a very good idea when it is warranted, prepared properly – and when the family is properly informed.

In my experience, too many people initially have thought that if they preplanned a funeral they had to prepay for it as well. This is simply not the case. I'm not exactly sure where this misconception came from but I have some good ideas.

Within the last 20 years, the government started allowing families to prepay their funeral expenses as part of the spend-down process to qualify for assistance. These funeral funds were exempt from asset allowance and could be put aside for future use without penalty. This was great for both the families and the funeral homes; however, good things often bring out the worst in some folks. Certain corporate funeral homes, as well as investment individuals, wanted a piece of this newfound cash cow. Thus began the push within the funeral service industry to try to get as many people to pony up as much money as possible.

Unfortunately, some misguided folks – or greedy ones – took this too far and now everyone is suffering the consequences.
The former concept of "pre-paying" has left folks confused about funeral trusts, whereby we put aside a sufficient amount of money to take care of expenses when a person dies.

I am a huge believer that a trust done correctly is one of the best investments a family can have in their advance directive portfolio. But a trust done poorly not only provides minimal benefit, it can actually instill a false sense of security and can harm a family at a time when they are supposed to be realizing its maximum good.

You need to increase your knowledge about true funeral trusts and I am determined to help.

A true funeral trust covers all the expenses that need to be covered and is held in an interest bearing account by a qualified third-party escrow company. Too often, I have spoken with a family being served by another funeral home and come to find out that they have exposure they never dreamed they had.

Consider this example. I was holding a seminar for a group of seniors regarding advance directives and funeral planning. After I concluded, we broke for refreshments. During coffee, a woman came up to me to chat. She said she enjoyed my talk and thought I was right on target with all I was saying. I thanked her and asked if she needed more information. She politely declined, saying that she was already pre-planned and pre-funded with another funeral home. I told her that she was very wise in her planning, but further inquired if she had a complete funeral trust. She said that she thought so, but what did I mean by a "complete funeral trust?"

I said, "You know, one that includes all the necessary expenses and not just the funeral director's goods and services."

"My funeral director said that his trust could only include things he was responsible for and that the other expenses would be discussed at a later time," she said.

"Do you know what the other expenses will be?"

"Not really, but I suppose there will be a few items to take care of."

After going a little deeper, I soon learned that "a few items" would include cemetery charges, church charges, newspapers, permits and fees, as well as a few smaller incidentals. Those few items, I was sad to report, would cost her more than $2,000 today and possibly more in the future. She had believed that she was all set.

What a shock it would have been at the time of her death to think that everything was all set and then have the family be handed an additional bill – for more than $2,000.

"What should I do?" she asked. "We had sold our house and had extra money when we formed the trust. We've pretty much spent the rest. Where are we going to find the extra $2,000?"

I remarked that she mentioned that her trust was in the $10,000 range. I said that I was sure that I could find a way to work with that figure to give her the services she was looking for, as well as pay all the outside expenses not presently covered.

She mentioned that it was with another funeral home and that she assumed that she couldn't move the trust. I said, "It's your money and you have the legal right to move it whenever and wherever you like."

Families sometimes need to reassess the relationship they have with their current funeral home when it doesn't fit their present wants or needs. She mentioned that maybe her present funeral home would work with her, as I was willing to do. I said that would be great, but I wanted her to ask a few more questions.

"I would ask them if they would be willing to take care of all the expected liabilities. You need to know what you are up against." The decision was entirely hers, but as constituted today, she would have had to come up with a substantial amount of additional money.

I heard back from that lady within a month of my presentation. She wanted an appointment to meet with me. The short of it was that after our conversation she spoke with her current funeral director and mentioned to him what I had said. He agreed that there would be extra money due and that it indeed would be in the $2,000 range, but there was nothing he could do. He also doubted there was anything I could do!

After reviewing her documents, I found a lot of fat in the first funeral director's budget; Expensive vaults and caskets, as well as a few fluff items that the woman really didn't need or want including premium memorial and stationery costs. Result? I was able to rewrite the trust to reflect the services she wanted as well as include the outside expenses. Same trust, zero liability, no more money due. Problem solved, happy family.

I routinely review other funeral home trusts for clients at no cost to them.

Just like getting a doctor's second opinion regarding health issues, funeral trusts can and should be shopped around. It's always a sound idea to have your funeral home trusts reviewed by a second independent funeral professional.

Few people realize that even though they may have established a funeral trust with a particular funeral home 10 years ago they can still update, alter or transfer that trust, if appropriate.

The family owns the funeral trust, not the funeral home. The funeral home is simply the administrator, not the owner. The family has every right to alter the trust if necessary, or, in cases where it is appropriate, to transfer it to another funeral home administrator. It amazes me that some funeral directors act as if they own these trusts.

Most families don't realize that they have this level of control over their assets. The money, both principal and interest, is 100 percent the asset of the family. If 10 years ago they wanted a certain type of service that is no longer applicable, they have every right to make changes and to reallocate funds for new and different purposes.

I routinely help families rebalance existing trusts to reflect new times and thinking. Oftentimes I am asked to review another funeral home's existing funeral trust to see where appropriate changes can be made. If the current funeral home is unwilling or unable to make the changes the family has requested, oftentimes the family will then transfer the trust for me to administer.

I have saved families a minimum of 10 percent of the value of the existing trust just by explaining to them what they are being charged for and what their options and alternatives may be. Not only do I help them to understand what they are being charged for but also, perhaps more importantly, I make them aware of unknown liabilities.

Part of my review also extends to making sure that the trust is protected and controlled by an independent third-party escrow provider. It is downright scary when I come across a trust fund that is controlled by the funeral home rather than an independent third party. I see way too often funeral homes that still hold trust funds in CDs and pass books that are under their direct control. Worse yet are co-mingled accounts in the funeral home name. The most disturbing cases involve funeral homes that invested the funds in speculative accounts. That is to say that they have been placing them in the stock or futures market.

Media has reported what has happened lately to those types of accounts. As I write this chapter Bernie Madoff is under house arrest!

We have also seen what happens when a good-hearted funeral director has access to trust funds and his cash flow gets a little tight. Families need to know their money will be there even if the funeral director is in Tahiti. It is essential to know where the trust funds are being held and who has access to them.

It is vitally important to get all the facts and to know where options lie. A little investigation and homework will not only produce a proper working relationship with your funeral advisor, but also probably save you a lot of money in the process.

Here are a few questions for families to ask the funeral advisor:

"How is the money invested?"

"What financial institution is holding the funds?"

"Are we protected if the financial institution or the funeral home goes out of business?"

"Does the funeral director have direct access to the funds or are they held in a true third-party escrow account as the law dictates? Are the funds transferable if another funeral home is selected in the future?"

The New Funeral Service: Breaking Tradition for Modern Families

When I began my career in funeral service some 35 years ago, designing a funeral was a simple thing. That's because we didn't have to design anything.

Back then, almost all funeral services were the same. For the most part, the service was pre-designed, and all a family had to do was drop in the appropriate name and off they went. There are several reasons why everyone had the same type of funeral.

First off, just about everyone was buried as a means of final disposition. In the 1970s, fewer than five percent of our client families chose cremation as a form of final disposition. Because most everyone was buried, people had limited options. Cemeteries, open during the day and only on certain days, had fewer times to schedule services with not a lot of room for improvisation. Most likely the family would be a burial family, and they would likely have a funeral procession. That meant fancy cars, limousines, hearses and the like.

Secondly, most folks were members of, or at least had an affiliation with, a mainstream or traditional religious community. The religious community affiliated with the family predetermined what the service was going to look like. Every mainstream religious community had a standard service, and the clergy had a predictable style that you could pretty much bank on. I remember working with several seasoned clergy and they had become so familiar with their habits I knew I could schedule errands and meals during the service just to kill the extra time.

Third, most folks belonged to a particular ethnic group. I grew up in the Greater Lawrence area of Massachusetts. Lawrence is an old mill town similar to many old mill towns of the northeast, with an extremely diverse mix of ethnic cultures. There were Italian, Irish, French Canadian, English, Polish, German, Belgian, Lithuanian, and many, many more. Each group had its own rites and ceremonies that, when combined with those of their chosen religions, formed a very specific service. If you fell into any of these categories, then the funeral director knew just what service was needed – not necessarily what was wanted.

Fast forward to 2009. The number of client families who choose cremation is close to 50 percent. The membership of mainstream religious communities is literally half of what it was in 1980. Moreover, the ethnic neighborhoods of early Lawrence are now composed of families with several different backgrounds because of multiple marriages, blended families and ideologies.

One of the main concerns I have now with funeral services is that changes in traditions have been lost on the average funeral director.

Most funeral directors had grown up in the 1970s or received their practical training from someone who did. What I've found is that these regular funeral directors are masters at performing funeral services that fit a particular model or mode. In other words, if you are looking for an Irish Catholic funeral service with burial as the final disposition, then these funeral directors are as good as anyone. They know the drill and can provide all the pomp and circumstance appropriate for a good old-fashioned sendoff.

The problem is, many of today's families don't fit the traditional mold.

- They are not involved in a church or religious community that would conduct a ceremony for their sufficient emotional needs.
- They don't have cemetery property, nor are they interested in purchasing grave space. If they've only been living here for a short time, and are not planning to have multiple generations in town to care for the grave after they are gone,

then cremation sounds like a good way to go.
- Most of these folks have such blended backgrounds that the traditional sendoff seems like a needless waste of money.

When a family operating with these dynamics begins working with a traditional funeral director, frustration can develop on both sides. The funeral director wants to utilize a traditional model that has, unfortunately, no meaning for this particular client. The client gets frustrated when the funeral director tries to create a funeral service for them that in no way helps them with their emotional, psychological or spiritual needs.

The sad reality is that even when a family is involved in a mainstream religious community, often times the creative process is limited to what the funeral director, not the family, feels is appropriate, necessary or proper. The desires of families who want or need meaningful services of remembrance get pushed aside or they opt to have no funeral at all.

Families not only want but need to have some type of service that not only honors the person who has died but helps them in the grieving process and allows them to say goodbye in a way that speaks directly to them. Many nonreligious families are deeply spiritual.

The challenge for my team is to work with the family members to create a unique experience that doesn't mimic everyone else's funeral.

Consider this series of questions:

"Are there any components of mainstream religion that we want to incorporate?"
A family may choose the services of a mainstream clergy or church even though they have not been active participants in the recent past. A person who has been sick or failing might have developed a relationship with a hospital chaplain or visiting clergy. Even though the person or family does not practice that denomination, the fact that a bond or friendship has developed makes this particular clergy person a logical choice to conduct a

meaningful ceremony. Nothing undermines a funeral more quickly than having a family instruct the funeral advisor to "just get me a priest or minister." If the clergy and family don't have the chance to bond, or if there is really no true connection, the message of the service is meaningless and the funeral attendees can't wait to get it over with so they can head for the mercy meal, the gathering that follows the ceremony. When this happens, the mercy meal then becomes the real funeral. That is when the stories start to come out and the remembrances begin to be shared. Mercy meal remembrances often carry more meaning than the actual structured funeral service. It's so important, therefore, for funeral advisors to listen, ask questions and create together with the family, a service that really speaks to all concerned.

"Do we need to look at special venues?"

If a family has been away from church for any length of time, then it may not be proper or comfortable for the family to use a mainstream church for the funeral. I've worked with families that thought it would be a good idea to have a church funeral, but had no connection to that church or religious community. They found the experience to be cold, uncomfortable or meaningless. Consider using the funeral home to hold the services – it sometimes makes more sense. For some families, even the funeral home can be cold and uncomfortable. The problem I've encountered here with traditional funeral directors is that they have overhead to pay on their buildings. If they're not generating revenue with their funeral homes then they are losing money.

Not all funeral directors either want to entertain or know how to entertain alternative venues. Many families either need further education on the concept of alternative venues or they remark, "I didn't know that I could do that!" The funeral advisor needs to really listen to clients and determine if an alternative location is right for them. I really enjoy working off-site with a family on an alternative location for the ceremonies. I've arranged services in libraries, music halls, function rooms, outdoor parks, VFW and American Legion halls, historic buildings, and many more.

"Can we truly personalize the affair?"
The family's preferences and comfort zones determine the ceremony's design. Often, this means more time and effort for funeral directors, but this is what we are supposed to be doing, creating a unique experience for each family we are called to serve.

I can recall dozens of memorable personalized ceremonies. Here are two examples:

One woman who died had an extensive collection of African violets. The family did not know what they would do with all these flowers after the ceremony. I suggested that we decorate the entire stateroom with all her violets. After the services, everyone in attendance would be able to take a violet home to care for as a remembrance of this remarkable woman. The flowers would thus be passed on and cared for and the service would be a unique expression of one of this woman's passions in life.

Another example was a young man who loved the outdoors, camping, hunting and fishing. We decorated the stateroom with all of his outdoor gear to the point that the room looked like a hunting lodge. We even brought in his all-wheel-drive ATV.

"If we don't have a clergy, can we still have a funeral?"
Too many clients, as well as funeral directors, think that if they don't "rent a clergy" they can't have a funeral. "Who's going to run the show if we don't hire someone?" Consider the concept of using a celebrant or coordinator to organize the ceremony. A family member or close friend usually qualifies and is ready and able to assume this responsibility. If in the rare case someone from the family can't do it, a funeral director may perform the role of celebrant on behalf of the family, to work with appropriate family and friends to create a ceremony that is unique and meaningful for their needs.

Even atheists and agnostics want meaningful services. "Dad was an atheist. He didn't want a funeral." Well, if Dad didn't want a funeral, the family still can honor his life with a ceremony or celebration that speaks to him as an individual. I remember one such occasion where a professed atheist had a wonderful ceremony conducted by his friends in the Marine Corps and a fraternal organization he loved. No church, no clergy, but a meaningful funeral ceremony nonetheless!

A funeral advisor who can exercise a little creativity along with ability to really listen to each client family can help that family explore all the potentials and the possibilities available to assure an appropriate and meaningful funeral event, unique to a loved one's particular wants and needs.

Burial or Cremation?

"What do we do with the body?"
-- 1930s gangster

As funeral directors know: we bury it! At least that's what we did more than 95 percent of the time in the early 70s. Thirty-five years ago, at least in North American cultures, burial was by far the most common form of final disposition. Not only was it culturally the most acceptable method of disposition, it was recognized by most major religious orders as proper.

In 2009, more than half of my client families are choosing cremation over burial. Other options are available as well, some more mainstream than others. Viable alternatives include:

- Purchasing a crypt in an aboveground mausoleum in many areas of the country.
- Body donation to organ banks or to research labs.

And then, as we learned from the highly publicized Ted Williams' case, some families don't choose disposition at all. They believe in the possibility that science will someday breathe new life into bodies preserved in cryogenic tanks.

Burial and cremation are by far the two most popular methods of disposition today. Pros and cons associated with either choice elicit several questions.

"Can we still have a funeral service with the body present with either option?"
This question comes up very often in discussion concerning cremation. Many folks are under the mistaken impression that

cremation is a type of funeral service. Cremation is a form of final disposition after a funeral service has been performed.

Many families are relieved to learn that they can have a traditional funeral with the body present and still have cremation following the ceremony. So, as you can see, with either choice, a full ceremony with the body present is available.

"How do our family's personal philosophies differ?"
You and your family need to be comfortable with the decision of burial versus cremation. It is, after all, a final decision. If Mom or Dad thinks that cremation is a good idea, but the kids feel better with burial, the problem needs to be discussed. Everyone should be on the same philosophical page if possible. This isn't always the case, but with sufficient education and discussion, generally a consensus and agreement can be reached that will be beneficial to all.

When I sit with a family to discuss ceremonial options and funeral choices, final disposition is usually addressed right at the beginning of the meeting. Folks often ask me my own thoughts regarding cremation versus burial. I let them know that I personally prefer cremation; however many of my own family are more comfortable with burial. I think that needs to be the basic overriding point here.

"What is the preferred or recommended practice of our religious community?"
For many years, the Roman Catholic Church did not recognize cremation as a proper form of disposition. Before the 1970s, most practicing Catholics would never have considered cremation, regardless of personal philosophy or circumstance. That has pretty much changed across the board and parishioners now have several viable options regarding final disposition.

It is best to consult with your clergy or spiritual leader if this seems to present an issue before an actual death occurs. Most religious orders make provisions for either burial or cremation options. Interestingly, most Asian and Eastern religions actually prefer cremation to burial.

It is always safer to know the options ahead of time rather than waiting until the last minute and then finding out that you don't have the options you thought you had. Check with your clergy before making final decisions.

"Is there existing grave space, and, if so, is it important to be buried with other family members?"
In the Northeast, many more families are generational than in other areas of the country. In other words, generations have lived and died here, and for the most part they have all been buried, usually in big family lots. Even if they are not all in the same lot, at least they are in the same cemetery. If your family has been used to this pattern over generations, cremation may be a little uncomfortable at first. Is the open grave space adequate for all family members that you want to be with? Is there enough room for your immediate family and not just for you? Is it important that you be buried with the previous generations, or are you looking to begin a new tradition for your family? Are you attached to the area of your ancestors or have you created your life in a different part of the county?

It is important to note that burial of a body is the final step in the burial ceremonial process, while with cremation there is still one more step to consider:

"What are we going to do with the cremated remains?"
This is where creative blending can occur. If a family has a cemetery plot but not enough room for many full body burials going forward, they may choose cremation and then bury the ashes in the family plot. This accomplishes several objectives. It keeps the family intact, with everyone still in the same family lot, and the cremated remains have been properly put to rest.

Cremated remains can be placed over or beside an existing burial. Ashes on top of a grave that has already been used do not take up open space for a full burial in the future. If only one open grave is available, one casket with a body will fill that up; whereas many cremains can be buried in an open grave as opposed to one body traditionally buried in a casket. Most cemeteries will allow multiple sets of cremated remains in a single grave; this allows ample space for several family members. Permanent memorials and plaques also can be installed in a cemetery, which is important to many families. The addition of the name of a loved one to an existing memorial or adding a memorial on the family lot helps to perpetuate the memory of the person who has died.

"How creative can we be with service times, locations and merchandise?"
In addition to alternative locations, a family can choose cremation services, which has the flexibility of nontraditional hours for the actual ceremonies. A cemetery has time restrictions based on their hours of operation. Cremation ceremonies can be scheduled Sundays, holidays, as well as during traditional times. A family has more flexibility with venues, ceremony sites and merchandise. Regarding urns, many old-time funeral directors either don't know or won't tell you that you have plenty of options for an urn for the ashes, that you are not obligated to buy something from the funeral home. An urn for cremated human remains simply refers to the container that holds the remains. The container does not necessarily need to be in the shape of an urn. It simply needs to be large enough to hold the remains. Not all containers are suitable or appropriate for all families.

I recommend to clients that if what I have to offer isn't necessarily suitable for their needs they are welcome to find an appropriate alternative. Some examples of urns that families have brought me to use are cookie jars, handmade ceramics, teapots and coffee pots.

Additionally:

- Scatter ashes in a favorite or sacred spot. Many families will scatter ashes at a favorite or meaningful site. Some churches and religious communities have scattering gardens for their parishioners.
- Ashes can be made into jewelry or kept in keepsake-sized urns.
- Ashes can be placed in a columbarium or niche at a mausoleum

designed to hold the remains above ground.

- Choose a combination of several forms of disposition. Families I've worked with may bury a portion of the ashes, scatter a portion and retain more as a keepsake.

I myself have plans to be cremated, and my ashes are to be divided into eight different portions. These portions will either be buried or scattered at meaningful places literally around the globe. One such stop will be on top of Mt. Kilimanjaro in Tanzania, which I climbed in 2005. Half the fun of constructing my directives is knowing that I'm arranging for my family and friends, if they choose, to see the world with me in tow.

One woman, an only child and caretaker for both of her parents who died within two years of each other, was given a special gift. Her parents asked her to scatter their ashes in Alaska. They knew she would keep her word and they knew she needed a reason to give herself a well-deserved vacation. Her parents provided for her travel expenses so that she could do something wonderful for herself as she paid tribute to them.

Finally, and important for most families, are the fundamental questions:

"How much does disposition cost? Isn't cremation much less expensive than burial?"
Burial generally does cost more than cremation. Even if a family owns the grave space, the cost to open the grave, dig the hole and install a liner easily can run $2,000 or more. The actual cost to cremate someone rarely runs more than $500. Even with an urn added to that figure and maybe a burial in a family cemetery plot, the cost rarely exceeds $1,200 total. So for many folks, cremation is not only philosophically appealing, it is cost effective as well.

The bottom line is that the decision has to be right for you. If you the "to-be disposed" individual choose one over the other for any other reason than that, then you will have major problems. Preclude those problems with preplanning and not leaving the decisions to others. It removes any doubts.

I have counseled many folks after the ceremony of their loved one, only to find that for one reason or another, they went with a decision that they were not comfortable with and now they are paying for it emotionally, and for a long time. Sometimes they made the decision based on costs rather than what they wanted. I will tell you that there are always ways to provide what is right and proper for the family. The fact that one may be a little more expensive than the other should never be the reason that a family selects a service that makes them uncomfortable. There is always a way to give the family what they need.

Please don't allow yourself to be talked into something that you are not comfortable with, whether it be because of price, family pressure or cultural bias. You have lots of options. Ask questions, choose wisely. It is, after all, a permanent and everlasting decision.

Ch 11

The Final Writes

More than just bullet points of someone's life, a well-crafted obituary is a mini-biography. Moreover, if you create your own "final writes" now, the process will move you to get busy with living.

Webster's defines obituary as "a notice, esp. in a newspaper, of a person's death, with a brief biography."

For most families and funeral directors, the obituary of the deceased is usually compiled during a 15- to 20-minute interview with a grieving loved one, placed in a format the newspaper generally dictates, and gets shipped off for publication in one or more newspapers. It all looks pretty simple and straightforward. That's what it has come down to for all too many families, funeral directors and newspapers. And it is unsatisfying for all concerned.

Consider that a person's obituary could be so much more if a family really understood the process. So many have missed the boat – many more can get it right going forward.

For most families, the obituary is one of the most important components of the funeral experience. Newspaper notices become keepsakes, routinely clipped out and saved by family members, who laminate them and use them as bookmarks and keepsakes. They are retained as family heirlooms, saved and passed from one generation to the next.

Why then do we wait until someone dies to craft something that is so widely treasured? Why do we only take 15 to 20 minutes to put something of long-lasting value on paper? Why do we just put down what a person did rather than attempt to capture who he or she truly was?

Begin giving this a little more thought, especially considering that most newspapers charge a lot of money to print an obituary. The charge for this content does not include editing or professional assistance in the composition.

By waiting until someone dies before writing the obituary, the result may fall far short of what it could be. Most large newspapers historically write obituaries on prominent people and archive them long before that person dies so that when the time comes and that person passes away, the paper can go to press immediately with all the right information already in place. These papers also tap professional writers to craft the obituaries as eloquent news stories and biographies.

CONCEPTUAL BREAKTHROUGH: Why should regular folks receive less attention or treatment than so-called prominent people? Get out the pen and paper or laptop and start to chronicle your own life now. Let your family know where it is filed. Be in charge of your own legacy.

An obituary done well serves several useful functions.

For one, it truly tells a person's story the way it should be told. Honestly, in summing up a person's life, shouldn't we spend time on who the person was? For most funeral directors, it boils down to asking a few basic questions and then sending the information to the newspaper along with a picture that may or may not be appropriate.

A standard obit will look just like everybody else's blurb after the routine questions are asked: "Where was the person born? Go to school? Do for work? What clubs, churches and organizations did he or she belong to? How about hobbies? Were they in the armed forces? Who are the family members?"

The challenge is that no one person is like any other person and those differences deserve to be captured. An obit is more than a passing thought and a standard format.

The story that needs to be told is, "Who was so and so? What kind of person was he or she? What made them tick? What were their passions?"

The second benefit is readers get proper and accurate information.

Families who wait to compose an obituary at the time a person dies are more likely to give incorrect information to the newspaper. I have met with countless families to help them write obituaries under duress. Many times when I ask the appropriate questions, the only answers I get are "I'm not sure" or "I don't know." Simple information takes on exaggerated importance. "Where did he go to school? Was dad in the service? I don't know what clubs he was involved in." Little details suddenly loom large.

To write the most basic of obituaries, accuracy needs to be a priority. These are, after all, going to be saved, laminated, and passed down through the generations. Accuracy is key to making this a proper piece of a family's history.

A vital component of advance obituary planning that absolutely needs to be addressed is the need to select the proper photograph to accompany the obituary in the newspaper. Way too often, if a family waits until the very last minute, the picture that is used to accompany the obituary is far less than flattering. People resort to using any type of picture when under deadline – driver's license pictures, employee IDs, snapshots from cell phones, backyard cookouts, The list is endless. If you can't find an appropriate photo, don't use one at all. Not to have a photo is a sin; to use a bad one is a crime.

I recently saw an obit picture of a woman with her breathing tube attached. If I were she, I'd come back to haunt her family!

Bottom line: unless a picture is selected with care and in advance, the choices available can be slim.

Personally, I know that I want to be the one to pick the picture that will accompany my obituary. I really don't want someone else to decide for me what they think is an appropriate pictorial representation of me. I've made sure that I've done that one myself. By the way, it's not a professional headshot. It's a well-focused photo taken while on an once-in-a-lifetime rafting trip in the Grand Canyon that portrays my passion and zeal for life. God willing, I'll switch that photo out every five years with age-appropriate photos that capture my spirit and personality.

A third benefit of pre-planning the obituary is it gives us a chance to write our own "autobiography."

I think that deep down inside each of us is that yearning to write our autobiography. The process can be rather fun and invigorating and very sobering as well. If not for anything else, it gives us the opportunity to let the rest of the family know who we are and what is important to us. It also gives us a chance to put down on paper what we think we are all about. This can be scary for some of us, but liberating for others. Either way, try your hand at you own obituary or ask for help creating it. The exercise is not only fulfilling but eye opening.

Another benefit of writing your own obituary is soul-searching: "What is my obituary missing that I have yet to realize?" Ask yourself, "Before the end of my life, what will have to happen to make me feel like I really lived a full life?" This is not about trying to get as many accomplishments in place before you die. It's not like the old saying, which goes "Whoever dies with the most toys wins." It's not about the quantity but the quality of the life lived. It's all about your personal "Bucket List."

Today, right now, is the perfect time to look at your life so far and ask yourself "Where do I need to go from here? What things in my life do I need to let go of? What areas of my life need more attention? If I died today, would I be satisfied with my life up to this point?"

I have personally used obituary writing as a way to reset my own personal compass, to measure where I need to make adjustments in my own personal journey and where I need to pay closer attention to others.

An obituary is so much more than a 15-minute interview with the undertaker. Begin to treat it with the proper respect it deserves. This is not only your own personal autobiography, but also as a chance to ponder and reflect upon your life to this point. Just make sure you include a good-looking picture!

Ch 17

Recovery

The period following the loss of a loved one needs to be spent working toward a new sense of normalcy or trying to create something new and different from the once familiar and comfortable.

It is important to acknowledge that life will change when we lose someone close to us. The intensity of the loss and the amount of time we will spend in recovery largely depends on who the person was and how close was the relationship with that person. The loss of a spouse can be much more devastating than the loss of a distant relative or casual acquaintance.

I've personally experienced many types of death over the years, and not just with the client families I've assisted. I'm talking about the death of people close to me, whether family or friends, that have caused me to go through a certain "recovery period" after the loss. Some of these periods were rather short and mildly troublesome and some have taken me literally months to work through.

The first noteworthy death experience for me was the loss of my grandfather. My grandfather was the reason I chose to become a funeral director. He was a gentle man who cared about people more than anything else. He lived to help others and he nurtured me as a teenager. When no one else cared about my thoughts or feelings, he was always there with a kind word of encouragement, support or timely advice. His death was a long time coming. He was stricken with several ailments that over the course of seven years just wore him down. I never really thought that he would die. Like many other folks, I just put the thought out of my mind and tried to go about dealing with life on a daily basis.

When he finally did pass, I was surprised to discover just how painful it felt not to have him, if not for anything else, just to talk to. I began to reflect on all the things I had wished I had shared with him. All the questions I'd wished I had asked, but now could not. All the knowledge he had that was now unavailable to me. It did help that we had a wonderful funeral for him. Many people attended and shared special stories of how he had made such an impact in their lives.

All this truly helped me turn my grief and sadness from losing my "mentor" to feelings of being blessed to have had such a special relationship with such a unique individual. The days and months passed, and I started to build on the lessons he had taught me. I started rebuilding that part of me that was now "changed" into something that I hoped would honor him and make him proud. I guess the greatest revelation to me was that even though I was immersed in funeral service and worked with people in crisis every day, I was not immune to the thoughts and feelings that make us all human.

The next time I experienced a transforming loss was the death of my father. Here was a man that had not only been my father, but was also a mentor to me in many ways. Our relationship was relatively rocky at many points. Most of this was due to the father/son dynamic and because we worked together and had very different opinions as to how things needed to be done. As the son, I was expected to submit to the father. As anyone who knows me would tell you, that wasn't going to be the case. We separated our formal business ties nine years prior to his passing. He was living a distance away and our contact with one another was seldom at best. He, like my grandfather, had several health issues that took him slowly to his death. In fact the last six weeks of his life were spent in a coma. I wasn't all that close to my dad when he did finally die. It did however amaze me that when he finally did pass, I was immediately overcome with tremendous grief, realizing the missed opportunities to connect, and with a sense of profound change. I think the grief and missed opportunity to connect is common with families who haven't been able to bridge relationship gaps, but the concept of a profound change came out of left field for me.

The change I allude to is that now I no longer had a living father. The man that had been part of the team that had literally given me life was now gone. I was now the patriarch of the funeral home family. There now was no one above me to fall back on. My mentors were now completely unavailable to me. I felt strangely alone and vulnerable. It mattered not that I had at that point worked in funeral service for 25 years. Just knowing that I didn't have that comforting layer of experience above me literally frightened me to death.

It took me quite some time to completely process that startling reality. The grief period went away more quickly. I rationalized my dad was in a better place, having gone through years of illness. The idea that the dynamics of my world, my relationships and my past were literally now permanently over kept popping up for almost a full year. I have since come to the comforting realization that all my mentors took me as far as they could and guided me to where I needed to be so that I could fly on my own. I know that the rest of the work is mine to do having the faith that I've been given the tools necessary.

Talking with a family about the recovery period, either before the death occurs or at the time the death occurs, is critical to shortening recovery time, lessening the intensity of the grief and minimizing any problems that may arise as a result.

Having the proper advisor team on board beforehand greatly aids in the recovery period after the event. Having the right mix of advisors and confidantes – and being willing to use them – makes a huge difference in a meaningful recovery. The funeral advisor is the person to speak with about any problem that may come up in recovery. He or she may not have all the answers, but they can provide the resource of identifying the need and targeting a strategy to address the problem. Counseling is a funeral advisor's forte.

A funeral advisor will listen to you when you're having a bad day and will understand what you are going through. The advisor gives the family comfort not only before and during but long after the death and funeral have passed.

Those with deep roots in their faith community hold their religious advisor in high esteem. Next to the funeral advisor, the spiritual advisor is probably the most important person in recovery. This person needs to be selected carefully and should be accessible and fully trustworthy. All other advisors should be selected with equal due diligence, not only for their expertise but also for accessibility and compassion.

Just talking about the fact that there will be a recovery period and acknowledging that there may be hurdles to overcome is a great first step in preparing for this difficult time. You can't predict what issues will arise out of the death of a loved one. Just knowing that issues will arise and having the proper people in place to call on in times of need will make the transition that much more successful. Having to identify, interview, establish trust and consult with advisors after and during crisis compresses the experience and prevents adequate mourning. Neither task, then, is handled well.

Make sure you have the proper resources, both financially and spiritually, to minimize your recovery time.

Most of all, pay due respect to your recovery. Something has been damaged, broken or taken from you. In many cases, all three have occurred. A loved one has been taken from you. Your family unit as you have known it is permanently damaged by the death. Your spirit and your faith have been broken by the loss. It does and will take time to mend. Like anything else in life, the more we acknowledge and take responsibility for our own recovery, the more positive the experience. "Time heals all wounds" may sound meaningless now, but in years to come it will become truer.

Every loss has its own set of dynamics and people grieve each individual loss in unique ways. The loss of someone you cared about a great deal will affect you much differently than the loss of a casual acquaintance. The dynamics of the relationship have a direct link with the person who died.

Early on in my life I never really thought about how someone's death would affect me emotionally. While the person was alive, if I was fighting with or had an uncomfortable or strained relationship with him or her then so be it. I had plenty of time to mend fences, to make things right. Time was aplenty to reach out, right that wrong, or simply to make that long promised connection.

During the past 30 years, I've let many opportunities to make things right go by the boards. I am always amazed at how little time all of us really have to make amends and fix the broken aspects of our lives.

I've also experienced this with hundreds of client families whom I have counseled. We are always going to make that call, fix that problem or right that wrong – as if we have all the time in the world. However, the reality is we don't know when we'll pass, so why take a chance of leaving relationships undone? Why not spend treasured time with loved one now while we have them, especially the elders?

Epilogue

In more than 30 years of working in the funeral care profession, I have observed one great truth. We are always in the circle of life, and hence we are always either planning for death, dealing with death, or recovering from having experienced a death.

It is important to realize that this dynamic is always with us.

It is also important to realize that the process is unique to each and every one of us. In other words, I will not experience the process as you would or how anyone else would for that matter. I share with you my journey only as a guide. Your journey may be very similar or very different. Many paths may lead to the same destination.

I think for those folks who don't understand the process and who don't plan, the most difficult part of the process can be the extreme highs and lows. When people don't understand and are not working on their process, these events hit them literally out of left field and will throw them for a loop. My hope is that you may now be aware of the process and do some kind of work on the various stages, so that when the time comes to be actively involved in one of the three areas, you will not be caught off guard. These life and death events will occur at some point in our lives. I hope that I have shared enough with you that we can do some good work together to attempt to minimize the trauma and upheaval.

May God bless you and keep you on your journey.